SYMBOLS OF
JUDAISM

Editions Assouline
26, rue Danielle Casanova   75002 Paris, France
Tel : 33 1 42 60 33 84   Fax : 33 1 42 60 33 85

© 1995 by Editions Assouline, Paris (*Les Symboles du judaïsme*)
English translation © 1995 by Editions Assouline
Second impression 1997

Distributed to the U.S. trade by St. Martin's Press, New York
and in Canada by McClelland and Stewart
Distribution for countries except USA and Canada:
Thames and Hudson (Distributors) Ltd

ISBN: 2 908228 35 1

Translated by Mimi Tompkins in collaboration with Liz Ayres

Printed and bound in Italy (G. Canale & C., Turin)

SYMBOLS OF
JUDAISM

By Marc-Alain Ouaknin
Photographs by Laziz Hamani

EDITIONS ASSOULINE

CONTENTS

FOREWORD

INTRODUCTION

1.
THE CALENDAR
The Hebraic year

2.
THE TALLITH
The prayer shawl

3.
THE TZIZITH
The fringe on the tallith

4.
THE TEFILLIN
Phylactery

5.
THE MEZUZAH
The parchment roll
fixed to doorposts

6.
THE SYNAGOGUE
The interior design
The *Minyan*
The prayer structure

7.
THE SEFER TORAH
The book of the *Torah*
Arone hakodesh:
the Holy Ark
The ornaments: the crown
and the silver plaques
The reading hand
The text written on parchment
The tools used by
the scribe

8.
THE SABBATH
The thirty- nine classes
The *Nerot:*
the Friday night candles
The *Kiddush:*
the goblet of wine
The *Halot*: the Sabbath bread
The reading of the *Torah*
The three *Seoudat*

The *Havdalah:*
the ceremony at
the end of the Sabbath

9.
THE CHOFAR
The ram's horn

10.
ROSH HASHANAHH
The Jewish New Year

11.
YOM KIPPUR
The day of Atonement

12.
THE SUCCAH
The Festival of Booths

13.
THE LULAV
The flower festival

14.
HANUKKAH
The eight branch candlestick
A tree of light

15.
TU BI-SHEVAT
The New Year of trees

16.
THE MEGILLAH
The scrolls of Esther
Purim: costume and carnival

17.
PESACH
The Jewish Easter
The *Seder:*
the paschal dinner
The main dish of the *Seder*

18.
LAG BAOMER
The pilgrimage
to the tomb of saints

19.
THE KADDISH
The prayer of the dead

and sanctification of God's name
The symbols of mourning
and consolation

20.
SHEBUOTH
The donation of the law
and the *yeshiviah*:
the rabbinical academy

21.
THE DIETARY LAWS
Kosher cooking

22.
THE MIKVEH
The ritual bath

23.
THE HUPPAH
The nuptial canopy

24.
THE KETUBBAH
The marriage contract

25.
THE BRIT MILAH
Circumcision

26.
THE BAR MITZVAH
and the *Bat-Mitzvah:*
the religious coming of age

27.
THE CLOTHING
CUSTOMS
Hats, beards, locks,
wigs, scarves

28.
THE KIPPAH
A skull cap

29.
THE TEMPLE
...and its memory: the western
or wailing wall

30.
THE MAGEN DAVID
The star of David

FOREWORD

to Dory

From Jerusalem to Bombay, Montreal to Johannesburg, Barcelona to Tashkent, with Oran, Algiers, Tunis or Salonica along the way, Jews all around the world follow the same rituals, celebrate the same festivitals, read and study the same texts, share the same collective memory, history and a similar sensibility. Despite the cultural diversity between their respective countries, Jews all over the world have one thing in common: Judaism.

In this book, we have set out to explore the fundamental aspects, rites and symbols of this religion, presented through images and a commentary that we hope will clarify their meanings and deepen the reader's understanding.

Every civilization and culture has its own rites and symbols which form the cornerstones of a collective existence, of material, intellectual and spiritual life. Every society adheres to its own rituals, its own way of inhabiting space and time, of living the sacred and the secular, its individual ways of eating and drinking, living and dressing, speaking, writing poetry, philosophising, making music, painting and being entertained. It is true that by living in the heart of a particular society, this purely ritual aspect of social organisation becomes habitual and is no longer questioned. The cultural becomes natural.

The origins of a particular practice, symbol or behavioural aspect can easily be forgotten or else they are never even learned. But the questions we no longer think to ask about our own culture, come flooding back when we look at another society or way of life.

The unknown and unfamiliar awaken our curiosity giving wings to the questioning process. We require answers to the basic and essential questions about Judaism. Hence all the rituals, symbols and particularities of this religion will be presented, analysed, and commented upon.

Clear observation needs a sharp pair of eyes and a questioning mind which is sensitive to the strange and unusual. For this reason, the publisher Prosper Assouline had the excellent idea of calling upon a very talented photographer who was not familiar with Judaism: Laziz Hamani, born in France to Muslim parents, with whom he spent several months in Paris and Jerusalem in synagogues and surrounded by objects that are an integral part of Jewish ritual.

This experience was more than a mere dialogue. Its fruits were a friendship among those who formed the team, and this book, the contents of which we hope will communicate the joy we had in writing it.   M.-A.O.

INTRODUCTION

MYTH AND RITUAL:
THE RHYTHM

I. MYTH:

THE FOUNDING WORDS OF IDENTITY.

The Jewish are a people of memory. More than the painful memories of the Shoah, more than the sum of Israel's many sorrows and triumphs, Jewish memory comprises both the real and imaginary events that make us who we are today. It is the root of our being, without which the tree of life would never bear fruit.

The collective memory of the Jewish people is inscribed in the Bible: first, in the five books of Moses, and then in the books of the Prophets and the Holy Writings. It is also handed down from generation to generation through the oral traditions inscribed in different collections called the *Midrash*. These accounts construct an identity around key values which become imprinted in the consciousness of each reader and listener.

The events recounted are experienced as mythical rather than historical events. Because of its mythical content, the event is no longer dated and its meaning becomes potentially infinite. The mythical tale recounts not only the meaning of the facts at the moment of their occurrence, but also the sum of meanings these facts have had for past and present generations, as well as the meanings they will have for generations to come. In this context, it makes no sense to wonder "Did this event really occur as the story tells us?" or even, "Did it actually occur?". The myth is not the "account of a true event" but the "truthful account of an event". This "truthful account", collectively accepted by the group, becomes a part of its memory - its "narrative memory", the individual and collective words which forge the origins of a group of people. The founding words of identity: this is the exact meaning of what we call myth.

Myths are transmitted from one generation to the next, first of all, through oral traditions. Stories are told around the fire in the evening or under a shady tree, where the villagers gather to listen to the ancestor who knows the stories and passes on the tradition. In the neighbouring village, the same story is told, but with variations. Some elements are added or cut out, the characters are uglier or more beautiful, kinder or meaner. The plot itself may follow other paths, turning the story into something quite different. There can be several, even contradictory, versions of the same event. But myth has no fear of contradictions. There are many different versions of fairy tales, for example, which in many respects, function like myths. The story of Cinderella has 345 versions (1). All these variations are distinct facets, different perceptions of the same event. Some myths are experienced affectively, others, aesthetically, and still others retain particularly ethical, philosophical or poetic aspects.

Although the work of oral narrative is neverending, at a certain moment in the evolution of each myth the oral form is given a physical form and incorporated into the written word. With the writing down of myths we witness the birth of "textual memory". The text belongs to the whole community. To write a text means to put its message at the centre of the community, at the disposition of the whole group. The strength of the great, written texts comes from their ability to conserve the multiple tones and approaches of earlier oral versions. The genius of the dialectic of the one and the many is conferred upon the Bible. A text possesses multiple harmonics and an infinite movement of meanings.

Textual memory, the second mode of myth transmission, is kept vitally linked to its oral origins through the interpretations of readers who try to recover the diversity of former variants beneath the unity of the text. In the Jewish tradition this body of interpretations, through which a single story will give rise to several, is called the *Midrash*.(2) Although schematic, it can be justly said that the work of the Masters of the *Midrash* and the *Talmud*, coming several centuries after the birth of oral narratives and their biblical renditions, was an attempt to recover in the subtleties of the text itself, between its lines and letters, the multiplicity of readings that flowed out of it.

The Masters were, in some sense, archaeologists of meaning, and very lucid ones at that, fully aware that the interpretations and narratives they propounded occupied the realm of possibility rather than truth, and sprung from imaginary creation rather than historical restitution. In the *Midrash*, the relationship to tradition is not an obstacle to creativity.

The remembrance of myth, through which the group's identity is forged, becomes in the *Midrash* a dynamic remembrance focussed on the future rather than the past. The *Midrash* is the continual renewal of myth, the continual renewal of the existential forces that forge being and enable it to reinvent itself outside itself.

The *Midrash* is the "memory of the future", memory which reminds us of our obligation to exist fully but without ever accepting the pure passivity of tradition. As Martin Buber puts it so succinctly: "For the generation that assumes it with a clear consciousness of its meaning, tradition is the most noble of liberties, but it is the most miserable enslavery for those who inherit it through a simple laziness of spirit."(3)

The *Midrash* is not concerned with telling the story the way it happened but with constructing a matrix of founding events which will have repercussions across the centuries. It is through the stories related in the Bible and reworked by the *Midrash* that the Jewish people recognise and identify themselves and receive, according to Paul Ricœur's elegant expression, a "narrative identity". The biblical text is an expression of an ensemble of stories and narratives which we call foundation myths, the founding words of identity. The narrative dimension of the Bible, called *Haggadah* or *Aggadah* in Hebrew (like the paschal narrative which is ritually read the evening of the Passover *seder*), provides the fundamental link between all myth and ritual.

Before examining this link, an important remark must be made. The fact that the Biblical text is in Hebrew constitutes a considerable advantage. In this purely consonantal language (consonants without written vowels) a word can signify multiple actions or objects. The Hebrew language thus dwells in the infinite realm of the incomplete, in an incompleteness that will forever remain incomplete and incompleteable. Word, therefore, becomes promise.

II. THE RITUAL: A GESTURAL MEMORY

The third way of transmitting myth is through ritual, which is the concrete expression and objectification of myth in the human body and gesture. Ritual is the "gestural memory" of the "narrative and textual memory" of myth.

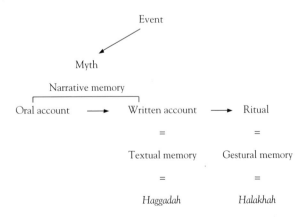

In the biblical text, as is also the case for the *Midrash* and the *Talmud*, myth does not exist without ritual, nor ritual without myth.

The dialectic of ritual and myth constitutes the very rhythm of biblical life and subsequently of Judaism itself. Ritual and myth fertilise each other; through their reciprocal tensions and constant interferences, they assure the life of the laws and the renewal of Judaic legislation and narrative. Narrative identity becomes twofold by adding an identifying behaviour; that is, by acting out the symbolic foundations of identity. By extension, the word "ritual" in Hebrew is *halakha*, which literally means "law". The biblical text is not only the place in which myth is enunciated but also the exhibition of the link between myth and the ritual that expresses it.

The most representative example is probably the episode in the life of Jacob, generally known as "Jacob's struggle with the angel". While crossing the river Jabbok, Jacob encounters an angel who does not allow him to pass. Jacob valiantly wrestles with the angel and overpowers him. The angel demands that Jacob let him go. Jacob answers that he will not let him go until he has received his blessing. The angel gives his blessing to Jacob: "Your name will no longer be Jacob, but Israel, as you have struggled with God and men and prevailed."

Victory opens the way to a "change of identity" and teaches us that man is not, but must be and that his existence is a duty to infinitely be. The poet Roberto Juarroz says: "Man does not live, he resuscitates. At each step, he resuscitates." And Erich Fromm teaches: "To live is to be reborn every moment." During the struggle, Jacob is touched on his hip and crippled. His lameness and the change of name are the strong points of the myth: Jacob and Israel! Jacob is Israel. The incessant movement from one to the other: this is the meaning of the word "hebrew" (4). The radical refusal of either a definitive identity or the fetishisation of the self.

Crippled identity and lameness continually remind us to escape the urge to classify, to close beings and things in the prison of names and words. Crippled identity maintains in man a constant questioning of identity so that he remembers that man "makes himself from unmaking himself", that the state of being constitutes the state of being "over there" — "somewhere in the unfinished".

Immediately after the angel's blessing, the biblical text states: "Because of this, the children of Israel do not eat the sinew." A dietary ritual was thus born which maintains the narrative of "Jacob's struggle", of his victory and his lameness, in our memory.

"Narrative memory" is therefore revived by "gestural memory", which is ritual. Every time we eat meat and stop ourselves from eating the sinew so as not to transgress this prohibition (that now extends to the hindquarters), we are simultaneously stating this imperative: Become! Construct yourself! Invent yourself! "Your perfection resides in your perfectability!" (André Néher).

In the framework of the study of texts, this dialectic of myth and ritual is extraordinarily fecund and creative.

The methodological rule can be stated in this way: each time we study a ritual, we must research its narrative foundation and vice versa. The biblical text then becomes formidably rich and original. It is in this spirit that we present the ensemble of Judaic rituals. We have equally developed other methods and themes that we will now leave to the reader and the viewer of these magnificent photographs to explore.

(1) Bruno Bettelheim, *Psychoanalyse des Contes de Fées*, Laffont 1976, page 407.
(2) The *Midrash* is also the generic name of the collections which brought these multiple interpretations together.
(3) Martin Buber, *Judaisme*, Verdier 1982.
(4) The word "hebrew" comes from the root word "avor" which means to go from one river bank to the other. It simultaneously means "crossing" as well as "fecundity" as the infant in the mother's womb is called "oubus".

CHAPTER 1

THE CALENDAR

HEBRAIC TIME IS BASED
ON THE MOVEMENTS OF THE SUN AND THE MOON.
"TO LIVE IS TO BE REBORN EACH MOMENT"

MONTHS ARE MEASURED BY LUNAR TRANSI-
TIONS, BUT YEARS ARE DEFINED BY THE
RHYTHM OF THE SUN. WHAT IS UNIQUE TO
the Jewish year is that it sometimes has a thirteenth month. When this occurs, the year is
referred to as being "pregnant". According to
tradition, Year 1 of the Jewish calendar coincides
with the creation of the world. This is calculated
as having occurred 3,761 years before the beginning of the Christian era. The difference between
the Jewish calendar and the Gregorian calendar
used in the West is therefore always 3,760 years.
To determine the Jewish year from a year in the
Christian calendar, subtract 3,760. For example:
5755 - 3760 = 1995; 5708 - 3760 = 1948.

Conversely, to calculate the Gregorian equivalent of the Jewish year, add 3,760. The year 1789
is therefore 1789 + 3760 = 5549, and the year
2000 in the Christian calendar will be the year
5760 in the Jewish calendar.

The Jewish calendar is governed by the
354-to-355 day lunar year, with twelve months
of twenty-nine or thirty days. The names of the
months of the Jewish year come from the
Babylonians: *Tishri, Heshvan, Kislev, Tebet, Shebat,
Adar, Adar Sheni (intercalary month), Nisan, Iyar,
Sivan, Tammuz, Ab, and Elul. Tishri* corresponds to

the Gregorian equivalent of September-October,
and Elul to August-September.

To keep the calendar year aligned with the
solar year and the rhythm of the seasons, the
eleven-day gap between the solar year and the
lunar year needs to be filled.

During these embolismic or "pregnant"
years, a thirteenth month is added, the intercalary month of *Adar Sheni*. This is a way of ensuring that *Pesach* (Passover) always takes place in
early spring, *Shebuoth* (Pentecost) at the beginning of the summer, *Rosh Hashanahh* (New Year)
at the end of the summer, and so forth.

Over a period of nineteen years, a difference
of seven months develops between the solar and
lunar calendars. Thus, in a nineteen-year cycle,
seven years will be "pregnant" ones: the third,
sixth, eighth, eleventh, fourteenth, seventeenth,
and nineteenth years. For example, the year 5755
(1994-1995) is the seventeenth year of the 303rd
nineteen-year cycle. It therefore is an embolismic
year. Holidays and feasts are held every month
except during the month of Heshvan.

– *Tishri* (September-October): *Rosh Hashanahh*
(New Year), *Yom Kippur*, and *Succoth* (the Festival
of Booths).

– *Heshvan* (October-November): the only month

of the year in which no religious event is commemorated.

– *Kislev* (November-December): *Hanukkah*, the Festival of Lights.

– *Tebet* (December-January): a fast marks the beginning of the siege of Jerusalem.

– *Shebat* (January-February): *Tu Bi-Shebat*, the celebration of the New Year of the trees or Jewish Arbour Day.

– *Adar* (February-March) and *Adar Sheni* (Intercalary): *Purim*, a holiday which commemorates the rescue of the Jews of Persia by Esther.

– *Nisan* (March-April): *Pesach* (Passover).

– *Iyar* (April-May): Israel's Independence Day, and *Lag BaOmer* (1).

– *Sivan* (May-June): *Shebuoth* (Pentecost).

– *Tammuz* (June-July): a fast marking the destruction of the Temple of Jerusalem.

– *Ab* (July-August): a fast marking the destruction of Jerusalem and of the two Temples.

– *Elul* (August-September): preparations for the celebrations during the month of *Tishri*.

Rosh Hodesh marks the beginning of each month. In the past, the *Sanhedrin* (2) determined the start of each month after hearing two witnesses testify to having seen the new moon or the *molad* (the precise moment when the moon reappears in the sky as a slender crescent, barely visible). A fire would be lit on one of the hills of Jerusalem, then on another, and another, until the signal had been transmitted across the country, and even as far as Babylon. When the Samaritans, a marginal religious group, began lighting fires at incorrect dates to deceive the

Jews, the Sanhedrin dispatched messengers from city to city. Finally, to clear up any confusion in far-away communities, the *Sanhedrin* named a second day to mark the beginning of the month. In 358 of the Christian era, Rabbi Hillel, the son of Rabbi Yehouda Hanassi, established a perpetual calendar, which eliminated the need to officially witness the new moon, or send messengers across the country. This calendar has been in use ever since.

In the Jewish calendar, day begins at nightfall, and draws to a close the next day at the same time, when three stars in close proximity appear in the sky. The Sabbath thus begins on Friday at sunset, and finishes Saturday evening at nightfall. The length of other religious days is measured in the same way.

The week is composed of seven days, mirroring the seven days of creation. The first day of the week is Sunday, and the seventh is the Sabbath.

(1) The thirty-third day between *Pesach* and *Shebuoth*
(2) The assembly of the seventy Elders

CHAPTER 2

THE TALLITH

THE *TALLITH* IS A PRAYER SHAWL
WORN BY JEWS DURING PRAYER AND AT VARIOUS
RELIGIOUS CEREMONIES.

THE EXPLORATION OF JEWISH SYMBOLS IN THIS BOOK BEGINS WITH THE PRAYER SHAWL. ACCORDING TO THE *TALMUD*, THIS EXEMPLARY rite is the key to understanding other rites. The spirit of God passes through the *tallith* via the written word. When words, particularly those conveying the names of God, are inscribed upon physical objects of the world, these words send vibrations out into the physical world itself.(1)

Words are more than tools for naming, tools which merely give access to objects. They also represent the life of these objects, as well as our own lives in relation to these objects. But only if we learn to listen to the vibrations of life which flow through the matter.

In Judaism, and in particular for the masters of the *kabbalah*, this life vibration is the name of God or the *Tetragrammaton* — the four Hebrew letters forming a biblical proper name of God, which often is inscribed upon physical matter.

The most exemplary trace is found in the *tallith*. The *tallith* is a rectangular shawl which can be made of any type of material, although wool, linen or silk is generally used. It is white, and has black, blue or multicoloured threads running through it.

The *tallith* must have four corners from which fringes, or *tzitzith*, hang.

In principle, the *tzitzith* should be made of the same material as the *tallith*. A silk *tallith* should have silk *tzitzith*; a linen *tallith*, linen *tzitzith* and so forth. But the most common practice is to use wool for the *tzitzith*, no matter what the *tallith* is made of.

Before wrapping oneself in the *tallith*, a blessing is said: "Blessed art Thou, O Lord, our God, Kingdom of the Universe, who hast sanctified us by Thy commandments and hast commanded us to wrap ourselves in the fringed garments."

On some *tallith*, the blessing is embroidered in Hebrew across the top of the shawl, which permits the text to be read. The fabric thus takes on the full meaning of the word 'texture'.

Some commentators (2) compare the black and blue threads to lines of writing skimming across a blank sheet of paper.

(1) Rabbi Nathan de Nemirov, *Liqoute Halakhot*, the relevant chapter on the *tallith*.
(2) *Menah'ot* 43b, *Nedarim* 25a, *Chavouot* 29a.

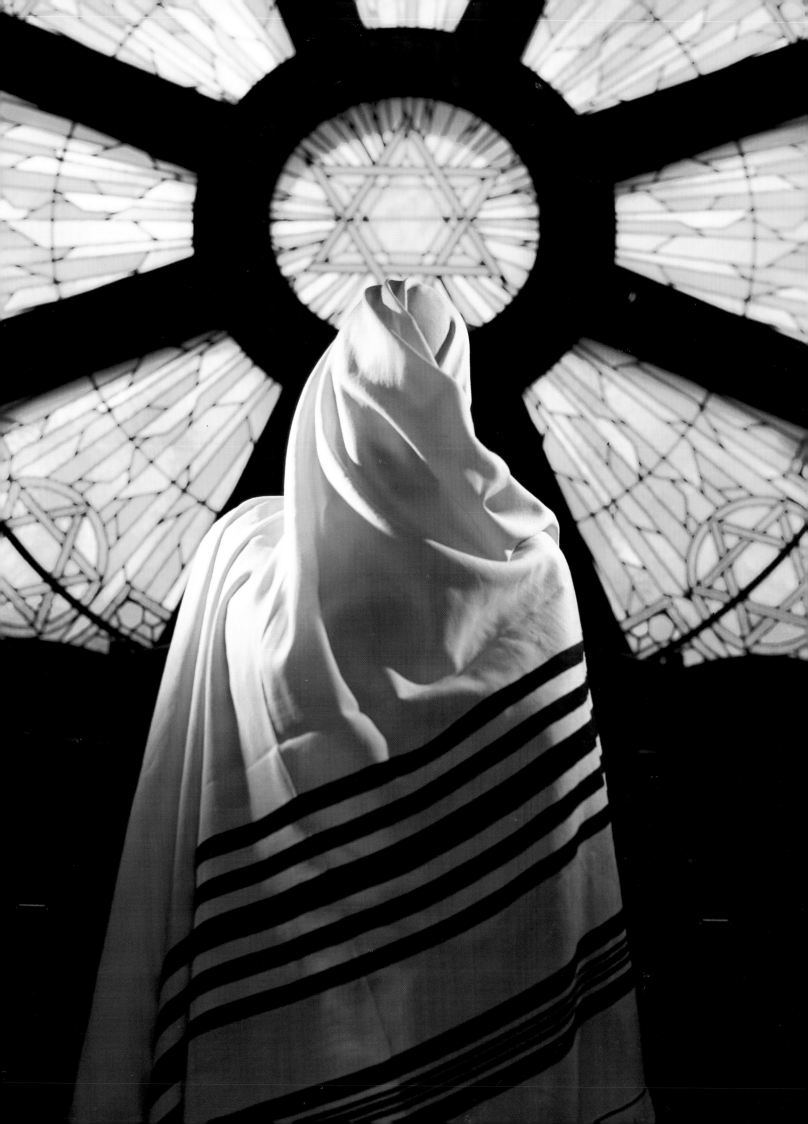

CHAPTER 3

THE TZIZITH

TZIZITH ARE THE RITUAL
TASSELS HANGING FROM THE FOUR
CORNERS OF THE *TALLITH*.

OBSERVING A RITUAL REQUIRES KNOWING HOW TO RECOGNISE THE DIVINE NAME IN ITS MANY FORMS MANIFEST IN THE REALITY surrounding us. This is very much the case with the ritual wearing of the *tallith* and its *tzitzith*, which consists of wearing a garment with four corners, each hung with tassels made of knotted threads. The number of knots and the number of times a thread is wrapped around the others in the tassel corresponds numerically to the name of God. There are two different traditions of how to knot the *tzitzith*.

The first is by writing the *Tetragrammaton* YHVH in its simplest form. In Hebrew, letters have numerical equivalents. The letters of this *Tetragrammaton* have the following numerical values: Y = 10; H = 5; V = 6; H = 5.

To make a *tzitzith* in this way, four threads are used, one of which is much longer than the others. They are fed through a hole in each of the four corners of the *tallith*. The threads are folded in half, creating eight loose ends, with one thread still being the longest.

Originally, the long thread was azure in colour, based on the colour of a species of fish which has since become nearly extinct. Over time, this tradition of one blue thread was lost, but it is undergoing a revival today.

The threads are tied in the following sequence: two knots are made, and the long thread is wrapped around the other threads ten times; another two knots are made, wrapped five times by the long thread; two knots, wrapped six times; two knots, wrapped five times, and finally, two knots alone. In this manner, the name YHVH is written, the *Tetragrammaton*, whose numerical value is 26:

Two knots; ten wraps (the letter *yod*)
Two knots; five wraps (the letter *hay*)
Two knots; six wraps (the letter *vav*)
Two knots; five wraps (the letter *hay*)
Two knots.

This totals 10 knots and 26 times that the long thread is wrapped around the others threads.

The second traditional method involves writing the *Tetragrammaton* YHVH with a variant, creating the meaning "God (YHVH) is One (EHAD)". The numerical value in this case is now 39, not 26, as YVMH = 26 and EHAD = 13.

The eight threads are tied in the following manner:

Two knots; seven wraps
Two knots; eight wraps
Two knots; eleven wraps
Two knots; thirteen wraps
Two knots.

This totals 10 knots and 39 wraps.

In the *kabbalah*, the number 39 is extremely

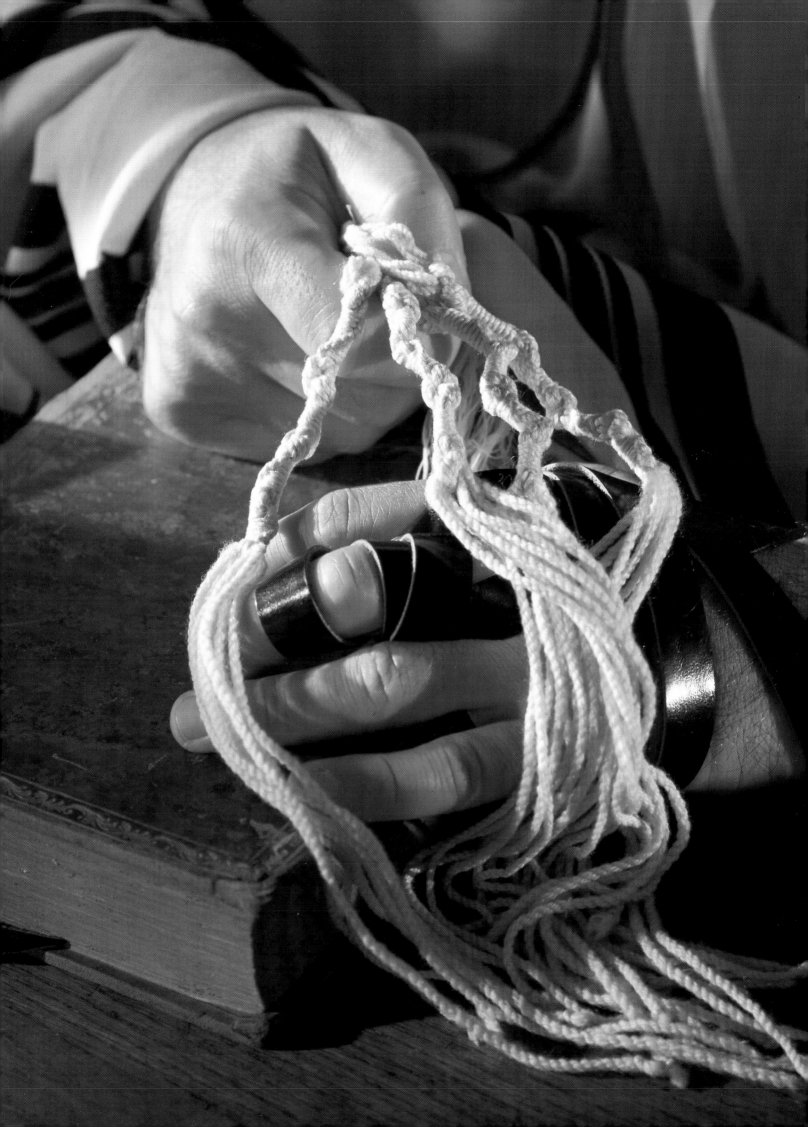

important. It corresponds to what is referred to as a "name in motion".

The *Tetragrammaton* YHVH representing God cannot be enclosed within the limits of a finite language. The letters within an alphabet can thus be put into motion, by turning each letter into the one which follows. An example using English can help clarify this point.

The word "time", for example, names a reality. To release it from its linguistic prison, each letter can be put into motion by substituting the next letter in the alphabet:

$$T \quad I \quad M \quad E$$
$$\downarrow \quad \downarrow \quad \downarrow \quad \downarrow$$
$$U \quad J \quad N \quad F$$

The word "UJNF" is the result of setting "time" in motion. By applying this procedure of alphabetic motion to the Hebrew alphabet and to the *Tetragrammaton* YHVH, we get:

$$Y \quad H \quad V \quad H$$
$$\downarrow \quad \downarrow \quad \downarrow \quad \downarrow$$
$$K \quad V \quad Z \quad V$$

It thus becomes the word KVZV (pronounced *Kouzou*) which has the numerical value of 39: K = 20; V = 6; Z = 7; V = 6.

As the prayer begins, the person wraps himself in the *tallith*, and enters a world of language in motion, so that the words he utters will carry him into a future which is creative and alive. For the being in motion, a language in motion is necessary and is thus written in the knots and wraps of thread in the *tzitzith* on the *tallith*.

During morning and evening prayer, a liturgical passage called the *Shema Yisrael* is read. It consists of three paragraphs taken from the Hebrew bible. Before the passage is read, the face and the eyes are covered by the *tallith* to emphasise the idea of "hearing", which is taught by the first word of the text, *Shema* — "Hear (O Israel)".

The rite of the *tallith* and the *tzitzith* is set forth in the third paragraph: "Speak unto the children of Israel and bid them that they make them throughout their generation fringes in the corner of their garments, and that they put with the fringe of each corner a thread of blue. And it shall be unto you for a fringe, that ye may look upon it, and remember all the commandments of the Lord, and do them; and that ye go not about after your own heart and your own eyes, after which ye use to go astray; that ye may remember and do all My commandments, and be holy unto your God. I am the Lord your God, who brought you out of the land of Egypt to be your God: I am the Lord God."

During the reading of this passage, the four *tzitzith* are held in the right hand, and are kissed each time the word *tzitzith* is pronounced. From early childhood onwards, men usually wear a small *tallith* or a *tallith katan* under their clothes. Sometimes the ends of the *tzitzith* can be seen sticking out from under the shirt. The *tallith* is kept for life, and even beyond. There is a custom of burying the dead in a *tallith*, after the *tzitzith* have been removed.

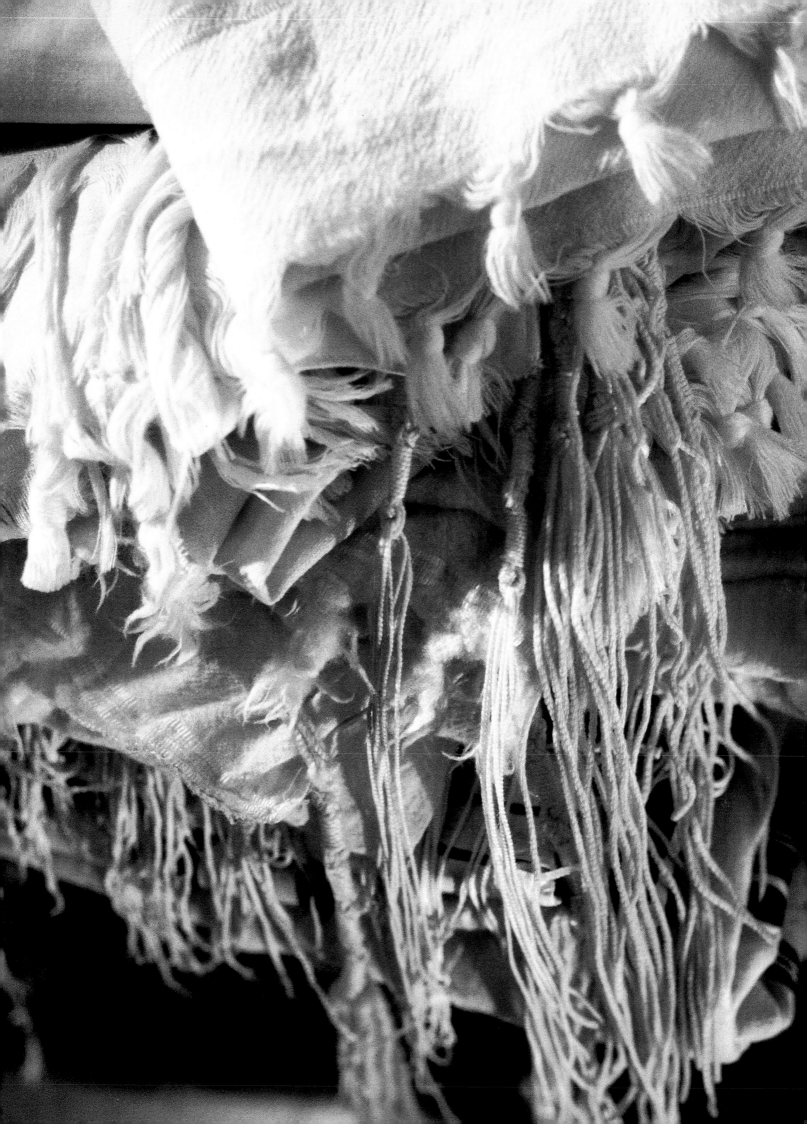

CHAPTER 4

THE TEFILLIN

TEFILLIN ARE TWO LONG, THIN LEATHER
STRAPS, TO WHICH A SMALL LEATHER BOX IS ATTACHED. ONE IS
WORN ON THE LEFT ARM AND ONE ON THE FOREHEAD.

THE *TEFILLIN* CONTAIN TINY PARCHMENTS INSCRIBED WITH TEXTS FROM THE *TORAH*. THEY ARE WORN BY MEN DURING PRAYER, except on the Sabbath and on holidays. One of the boxes is attached to the left arm by wrapping the strap around it seven or eight times. The other box is worn on the forehead, positioned between the eyes, and the strap is wrapped around the head and knotted. The straps hang down over the shoulders.

Inside these boxes are tiny parchments: one for the arm, and four different ones for the head. The single parchment for the arm bears four texts, while the four parchments for the head each bear one text. These texts are *Exodus* 13:1-10; 13: 11-16; *Deuteronomy* 6: 4-9; 11: 13-21 (1).

The theme of "memory" recurs in these texts like a leitmotiv: "You will wear the *tefillin* like a sign upon thy hand and a memorial between thine eyes". The Hebrew word *zikaron*, or memory, comes from the root Z.K.R., which also means "masculine."

The ritual of the *tefillin* carries with it the idea of *zikaron*, memory and memorial. The four texts of the *tefillin* all express the idea of this "memorial" between the eyes. But the second text uses the mysterious word *Totafot* instead of *zikaron*

— mysterious because it is not a Hebrew word. Rashi has ascertained that *Totafot* is a word... from Africa! *Tot* means "two" as does *fot*, in an African language. Why is the word "memory" written in a foreign language, in this case in an African language? It could be a fundamental way of teaching that one person's memory exists through the remembrance of another. It demonstrates openness to other languages and other cultures, a willingness to regard the African as a brother.

This is not a reinforcement of identity by seeking the roots which enclose us, but a questioning of our identity. To remember is to be open, to question.

Rabbi Nahman of Bratslav said: "There is only memory in the world which is to come", or, in a more incisive formula, "remember your future". The future of each person is manifest in the memory of another's existence, which opens us to dialogue and creativity. Wrapped in his *tallith*, language in motion, and bearing the *tefillin*, remembering the future, a man begins his day by a prayer which fills him with creative energy and gives him support in his material, spiritual and intellectual life. In this ritual, the same idea encountered in the *tallith* surfaces — the inscription of language, specifically the names of God, upon

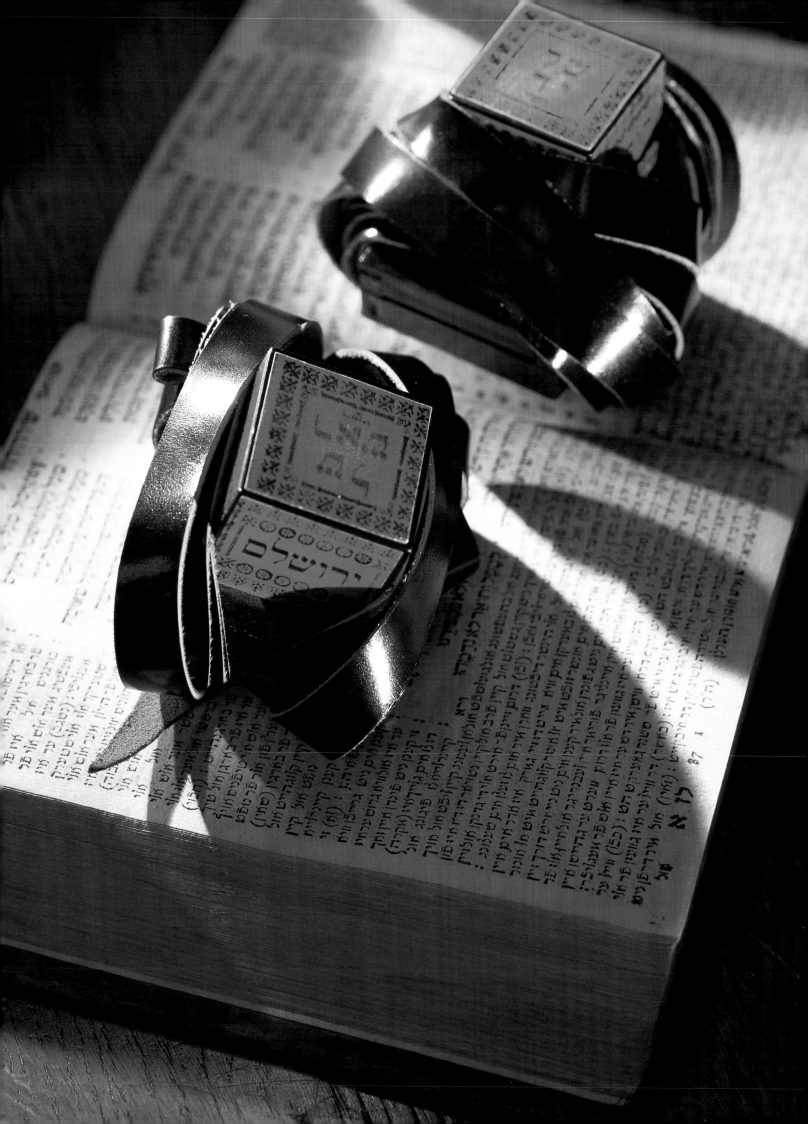

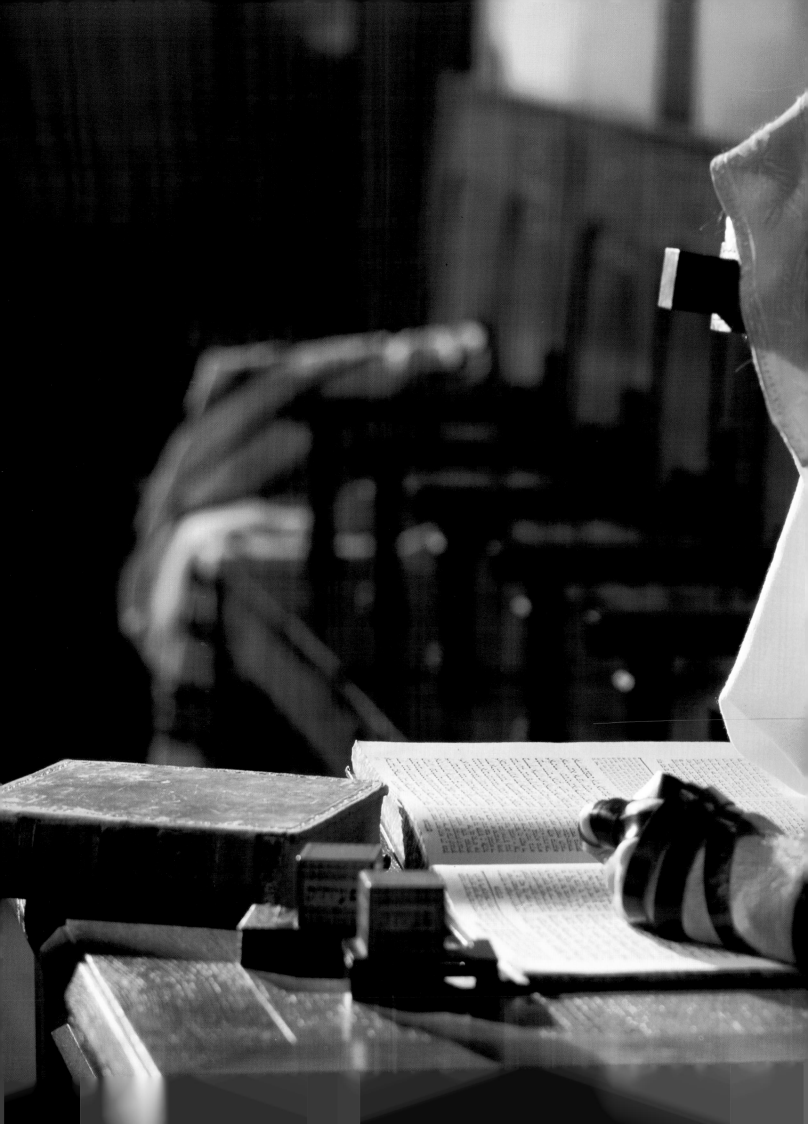

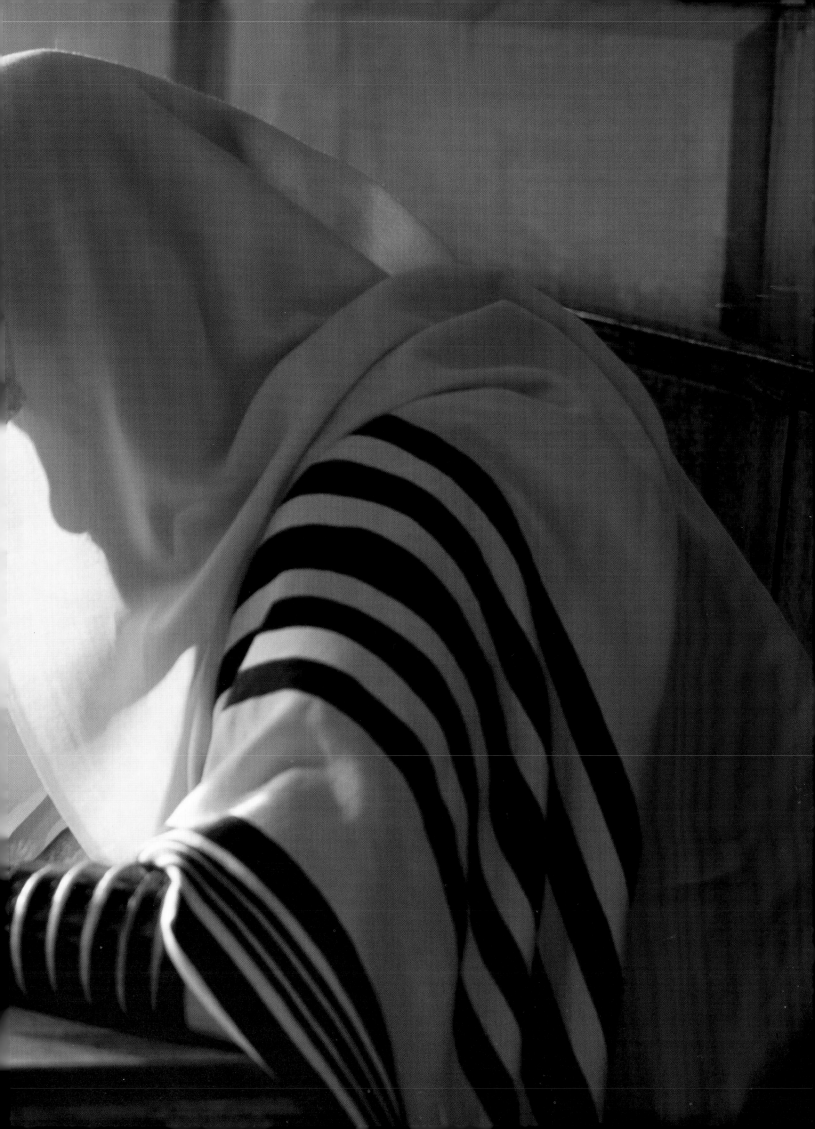

the texture of reality; the written word expressed on and by ritual objects.

Two ways of writing the letter *shin* are inscribed on the *tefillin* worn on the head, one having three strokes, the other four:

The knot, made from the thin leather straps tied on the head, form the letter *daleth*, while the knot by the box on the arm forms the letter *yod* at the box.

letter *Daleth*   letter *Yod*

These three letters form the word *Shaddai*, which is one of the names of God. The *Talmud* gives several explanations for this name. The first divides *Shaddai* into *Che-dai*, the abbreviation of a longer expression, *Mi-cheamar leolamo dai* — "he who says to his world 'that's enough'."

God regulates the entropy of the world, introducing limits to the reality of things. Through the rite of the *tefillin*, man transposes the feeling of his finite nature onto his own body. It is a lesson in humility and modesty which balances the idea of opening up the self, mentioned at the beginning of this chapter.

The second explanation analyses the etymology of the word *Shaddai*: *Chad* means a woman's breast, which is both an erotic object and a nourishing one. *Shaddai* literally means "my breasts". It is a word used by a woman when speaking about her body.

According to the *Talmud* (*Yoma* 54a), these breasts are not exposed in a pure and direct nudity, but are covered with a veil. This is not to hide them, but to make them both visible and invisible at the same time. This vision of the breasts, an oddly erotic one, is the vision which the High Priest would have the day of *Kippur* in the most sacred place in the Temple.

Transcendence and eroticism? Eroticism is defined here by that which simustaneously reveals and hides itself, a game of "visible, invisible". Thus, one could say that God appears in an erotic way, both visible and invisible. God completely unveiled would be an idol; entirely veiled, he would be absent.

Here, the "visible and the invisible" is coupled with the "graspable and ungraspable". The text cannot be totally grasped, cannot act as an idol. Its meaning remains enigmatic, a vehicle for time and transcendence. The eroticism of the *Shaddai* reverses the "limitative" aspect of the *Shaddai* which, according to the first explanation, means the "boundary" the "that's enough".

The *tefillin* allows man in prayer to become conscious of his ability to open up to the infinite, despite the finite nature of his material being and his humanness.

(1) The order of the texts can vary according to tradition. We are following the tradition of Rashi.

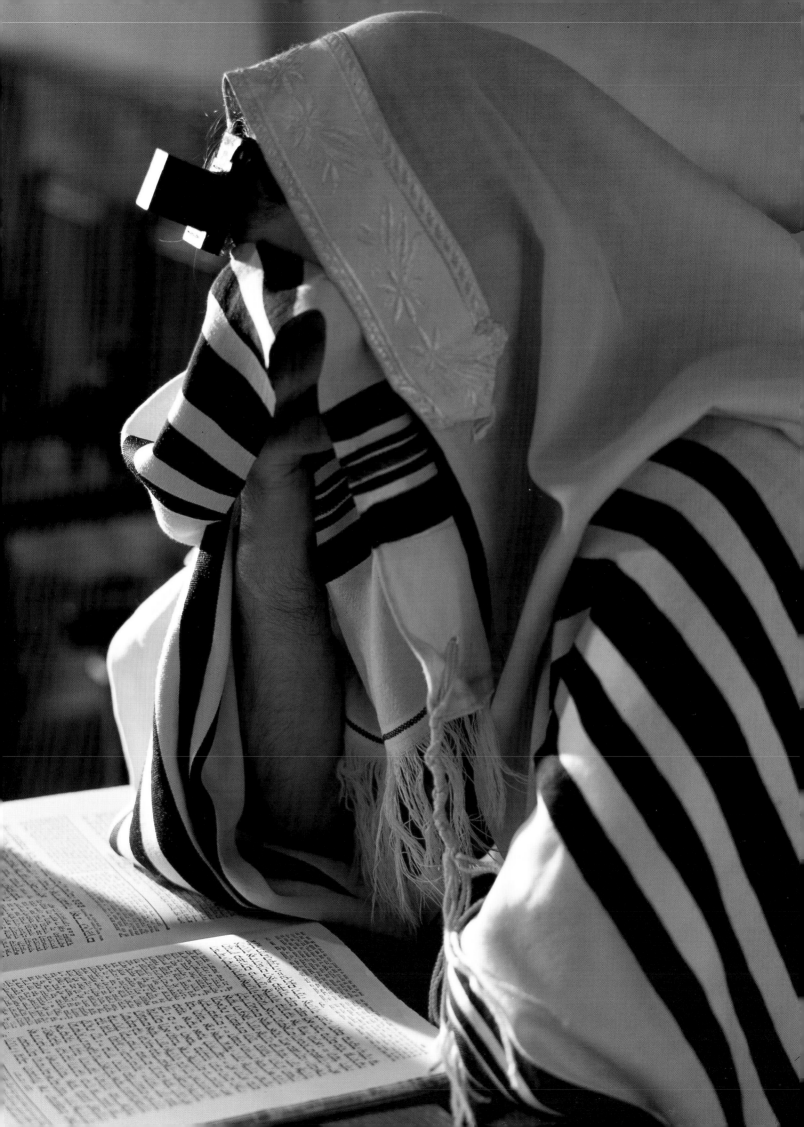

CHAPTER 5

THE MEZUZAH

THE *MEZUZAH* IS A SMALL PIECE OF
PARCHMENT ON WHICH SEVERAL PASSAGES FROM THE TORAH
HAVE BEEN WRITTEN. IT IS AFFIXED TO THE RIGHTHAND
SIDE OF THE ENTRANCE TO THE HOUSE.

THE *MEZUZAH* PLAYS A SYMBOLIC ROLE AS A PROTECTOR AND AS A REMINDER TO FOLLOW A CERTAIN ETHIC OF REMAINING "ON THE way" as a state of being. The *mezuzah* is a piece of parchment on which the first paragraphs of the *Shema* are written (*Deuteronomy*, 6:4-9, and 11:13-21). The parchment is rolled up and inserted into a tube usually of wood or metal, but it can be made of other types of material. The *mezuzah* is fixed onto the front doorpost, on the right hand side, a third of the way down from the lintel. If the door is too tall, the *mezuzah* should be placed at a reachable level.

Before affixing the *mezuzah* , the following blessing is given: "Blessed is our eternal God of the universe, who hast commanded us to fix the *mezuzah*".

In the *Shema*, the word *mezuzah* also means doorpost. Affixing the *mezuzah* to all the doors in the house (except the doors to the lavatories and the bathroom) is a positive commandment which is written in *Deuteronomy* — "And thou shalt write them upon the doorposts of thy house and upon thy gates". (*Deuteronomy* 6:9). The *mezuzah* is put up only in permanent houses, not in temporary dwellings, such as the *succah*.

The *mezuzah* should be put in place by the owner or the person renting the home thirty days after moving in. In Israel, they must be put up immediately. Women must also take part.

If *mezuzot* are fixed to several doorposts in a house, only one blessing need be given, as long as the intention to do so is stated before the first one is put up. The *mezuzah* is written by a Sofer, a scribe who copies the *Sefer Torah* and the *tefillin*, as well as the *mezuzot*. A *mezuzah* is not valid when printed by a machine nor is it acceptable if one letter in the text has been erased.

The *Talmud* recounts the tale of a man named Artaban who sent a very precious stone to Rabbi Yehouda the Prince. To thank him, Rabbi Yehouda the Prince sent Artaban a *mezuzah*. Artaban was greatly surprised to receive the present in return and he replied, "I sent you a valuable stone and you thank me with a simple piece of parchment?" Rabbi Yehouda replied that the parchment had more value than all precious stones put together. Artaban did not answer, but deep down he couldn't help but think that the rabbi had sold him short.

Several years later, Artaban's daughter fell ill. One after another, different doctors tried to help, but each failed.

Then Artaban remembered the rabbi's

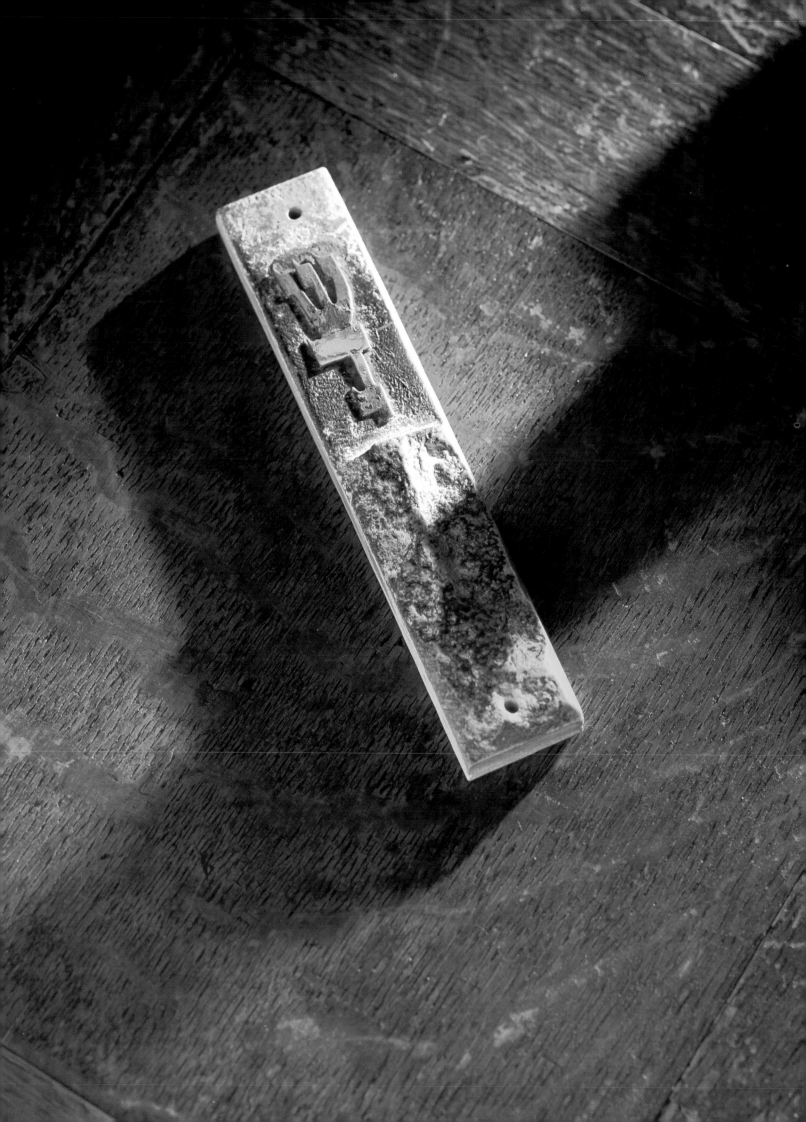

words. He affixed the *mezuzah* to the doorpost of his daughter's bedroom... and she recovered!

A look at the structure of the *mezuzah* allows for a better understanding of the meaning of this rite. As with the *tefillin*, this is a text which is not meant to be opened and read. The parchment is rolled up and enclosed in a tube. It is therefore "visible-invisible", "readable-unreadable", which is the same erotic form that was explained in the previous chapter.

The proof of this, is that the name *Shaddai* is the word written on the visible, readable side of the parchment. On the back, further words are written upside down...

To read it correctly, the head must be turned upside down. In the chapter on the *tallith*, it was explained how God's name is put into motion by moving the letters forward in the alphabet.

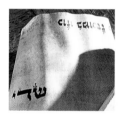

Shaddai and *Kouzou* on the *mezuzah*

Grammatically, the *Tetragrammaton* YVMH means the past (HYH), the present (HVH) and the future (YHH). The four letters of the *Tetragrammaton* therefore enable the writing of these three modalities in time that is alive, that is of life, held between memory and hope. Affixed to the doorpost of a home, the *mezuzah* is a reminder to man that he has come a long way,

but that the voyage does not end here, and that he must continue to reinvent himself.

The *mezuzah* represents this idea of "setting into motion" and it also suggests how to incite it through language in motion, the key example being that of *Kouzou*.

Man is a creature of language who relates to time, that is to say he lives through a living, breathing language, which is subject to study and interpretation. By questioning single interpretations, he opens words up to multiple and diverse meanings, and in doing so, opens himself up, thus freeing himself from any confinement and sense of lassitude, so as to be able to constantly reinvent himself, to live and be reborn at every instant.

The rite of the *mezuzah* is an invitation to perpetual motion. It is interesting to note that a good number of the texts from the *Talmud* and the *Midrash* begin with this idea of being "on the way", for example, "The Rabbi and the Rabbi Hiya were on their way..."

In fact, every text in the *Talmud* begins with the idea of being "on the way", even if that isn't the specific expression used.

The *Talmud*, the *Midrash* and the *Kaballah* all contain "thought in motion" — men who think while walking and follow the truth of the path. Without a doubt at all, this is one of the meanings of the verse: "And thou shalt teach them diligently... and when thou walkest by the way." (*Deuteronomy* 6:7)

The process of travelling, the way, is everything. We are closer to the place we seek when

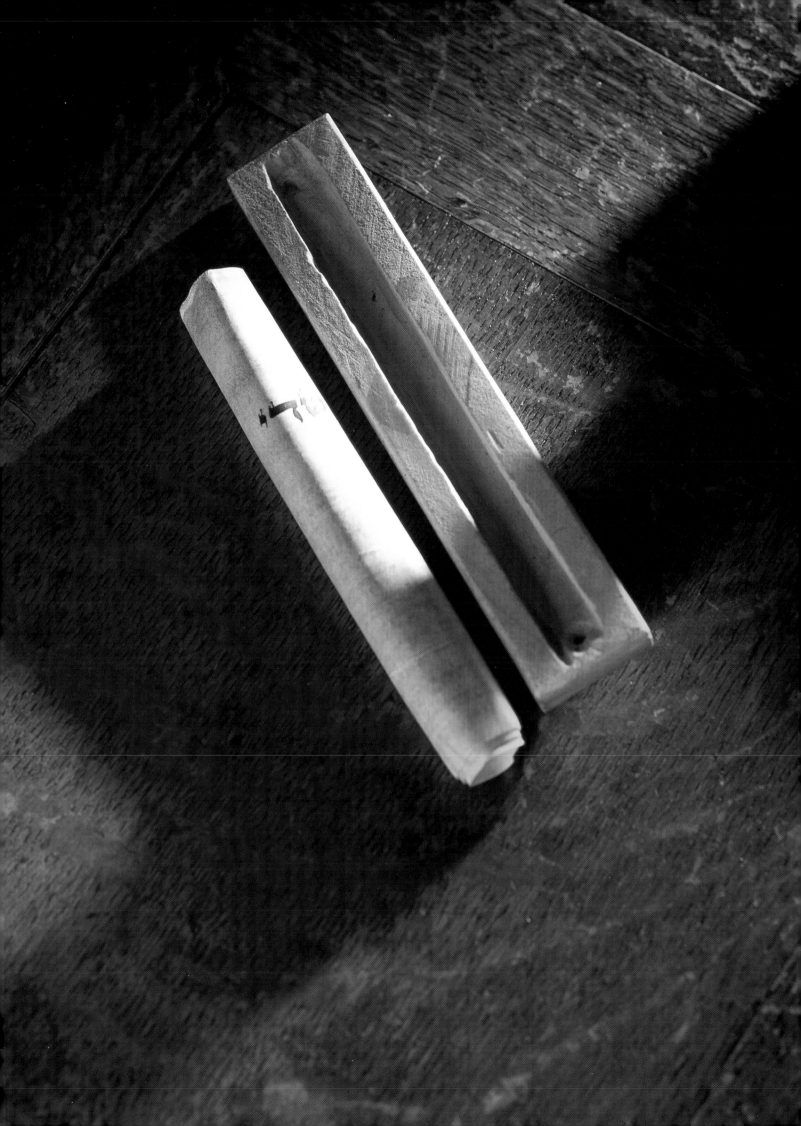

we are on the way there, than when we are convinced we have arrived, and all that remains is to settle there. As Edmond Jabes wrote: "Never forget that you are a traveller in transit."

The word "way" doesn't necessarily have a spatial meaning. It is not a stroll through a forest or field of our wandering thoughts. It doesn't lead us from one place to another. It is the passage, the movement, of thought itself.

Being on the way sets one in motion, triggers questioning, consideration. It invites and disturbs, incites and appeals. Man "on his way" does not just apply to a Jew, but to man in general.

In one of the most beautiful texts written about the Jewish being, inspired by André Neher, Maurice Blanchot expands and develops this central idea of Judaism. The following is a synopsis of his principal ideas:

"What does it mean to be Jewish? Why does this state exist? It exists so that the idea of being 'on the way' as a movement, and a just movement, may exist. It exists so that along the way and by the way, the experience of that which is strange and unknown may coalesce around us and be experienced in an irreducible way. It exists so that we learn how to speak through the authority of this experience.

To be 'on the way' is to be perpetually ready to move on; it is a requirement to pull oneself up and away, an affirmation of the truth of nomadic existence.

In this way, the Jew differentiates himself from the pagan. To be pagan is to fix oneself somewhere, fix oneself to the ground to a certain extent, establish oneself through a pact with permanency which authorises the sojourn and certifies the certitude of territory. Being on the way, being nomadic is a response to a way of being which possession does not satisfy. To put oneself on the way, to be on the way, is already the meaning of the words heard by Abraham: 'Leave your birthplace, your kin, your home.' "

It is important to emphasise that the meaning of these words is positive. Blanchot continues: "If we put ourselves on the way and wander aimlessly, is it because we are condemned to exclusion and barred from having a dwelling because we are excluded from the truth? Isn't it rather that this wandering represents a new way of relating to 'the truth'?

Rather than an eternal deprivation of a dwelling place, isn't this nomadic existence an authentic way of living, of residing, which does not bind us to a determination of place, nor secure us to a reality which is already justified, certain and permanent?

It is as though the sedentary state is the goal for all behaviour! As though truth itself were sedentary!

It is important to leave one's home, to come and to go as a way of affirming that life is in fact a journey."

And this is the message of the *mezuzah*. (1)

---

(1) The mezuzah is fixed slanting to the left, representing the movement of a man's shoulders and arms as he walds.

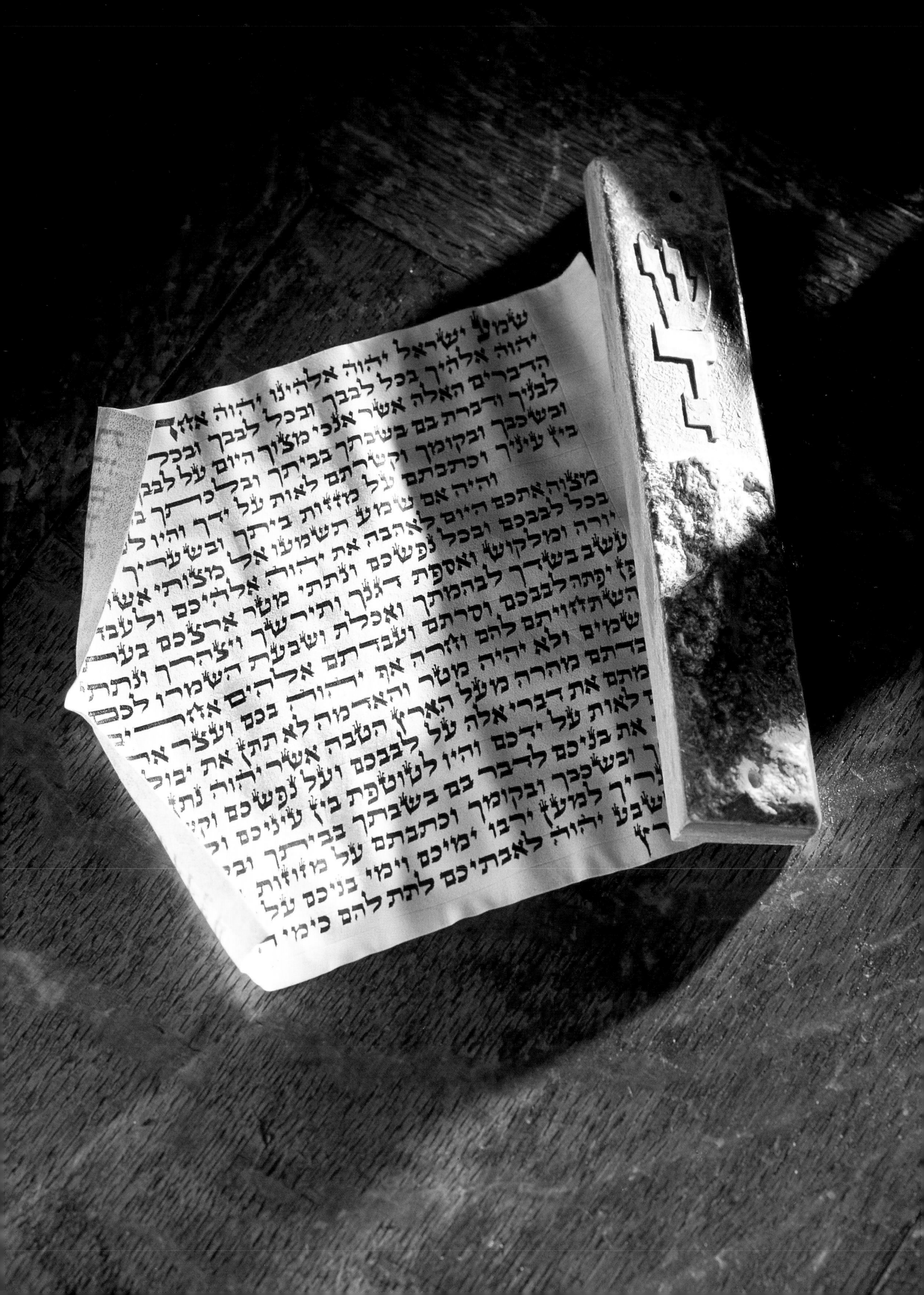

שמע ישראל

CHAPTER 6

THE SYNAGOGUE

THE SYNAGOGUE IS
ESSENTIALLY A GATHERING PLACE.

THE ARCHITECTURAL DESIGN OF THE SYNA-GOGUE IS SIMPLE AND SPARE. IN FACT, IT IS NOT THE BUILDING ITSELF THAT IS IMPORTANT but the act of gathering together.

There are three daily prayers: *shacharith* in the morning; *minchah* in the afternoon; *maariv* in the evening. Along with the *Beth Hamidrash*, or House of Study (1), the synagogue is the central location of communal Jewish life. Three times a day, a *minyan* of at least ten men gather to pray in the synagogue.

The historical origins of the synagogue are imprecise, but the idea of several members of the community meeting on a regular basis has always existed. It developed most specifically during the time of the Babylonian exile and of the prophet Ezekiel, following the destruction of the first Jerusalem Temple, in 586 before the common era. The role of the synagogue became vital after the second Temple was destroyed. The ritual sacrifices offered at the Temple were replaced by insti-tutionalised prayers, whose texts were written in their definitive form.

It is even said that the synagogue inherited the holiness of the Temple. Respect for the syna-gogue is required, and behaviour within its walls must therefore be decent. Drinking, eating and sleeping are not permitted inside the synagogue. However, when a House of Study also serves as a synagogue, eating and sleeping here is considered normal behaviour.

Originally, synagogues were of a very simple architectural design. In countries where anti-Semitism was rife, Jews did their best to construct very discrete synagogues in the Jewish quarters, with facilities for the *mikveh*, or ritual bath, the community hall and other communal institutions nearby. Despite restrictions imposed on the con-struction of synagogues, many were veritable gems in countries such as Italy (most notably in Venice and Rome), Spain, Poland, Egypt (in Alep), or Tunisia. In the absence of current restrictions on size, the architectural design of the synagogue has become quite diverse, and much attention is de-voted to aesthetics.

I. THE INTERIOR ARCHITECTURE

The most important object inside a synago-gue is the *Sefer Torah*, the book of the *Torah*. It sits in the *Aron Hakodesh*, the Holy Ark, located at one end of the synagogue, taking up all or part of the east wall. The Ark is turned towards Jerusalem, and elevated upon a platform (see chapter 20 on the *Sefer Torah*).

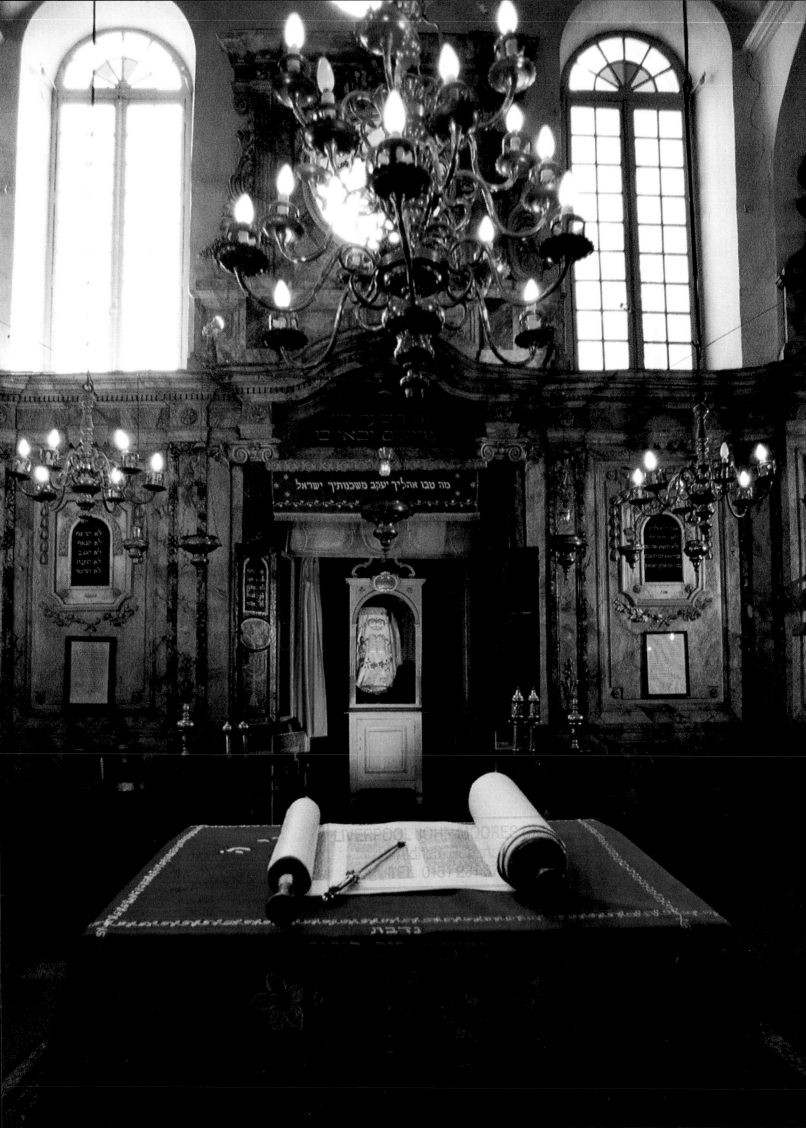

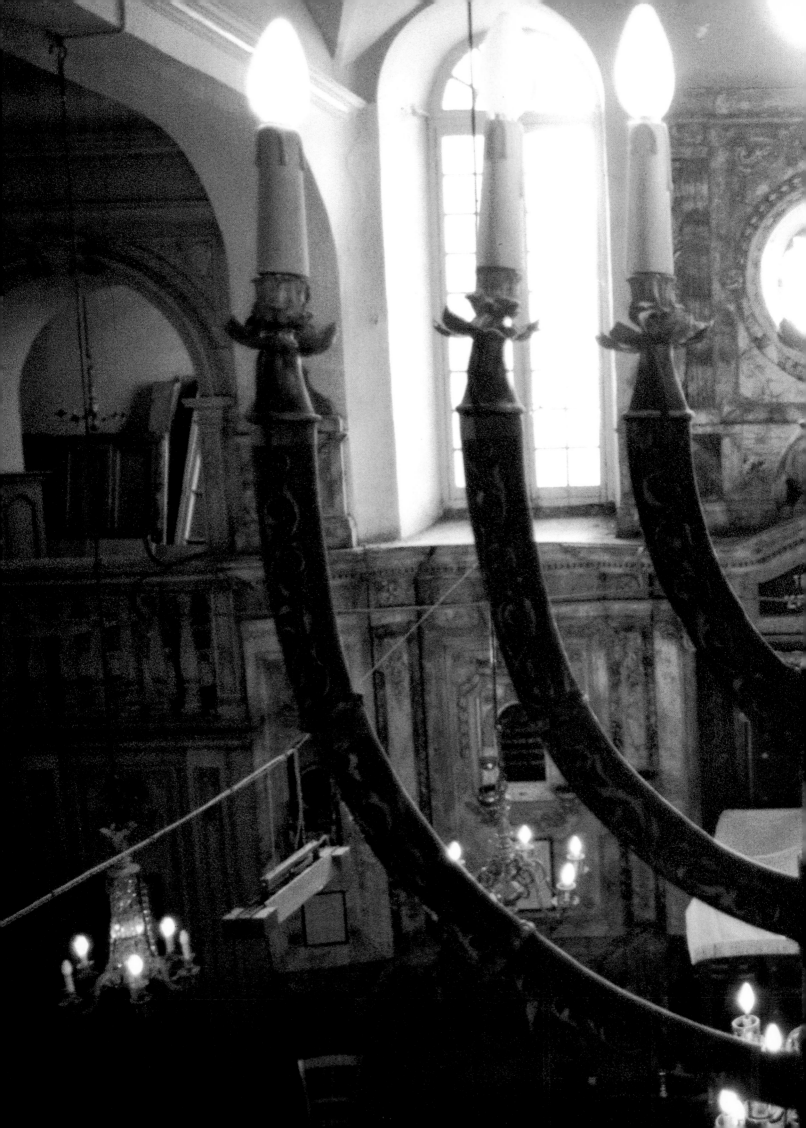

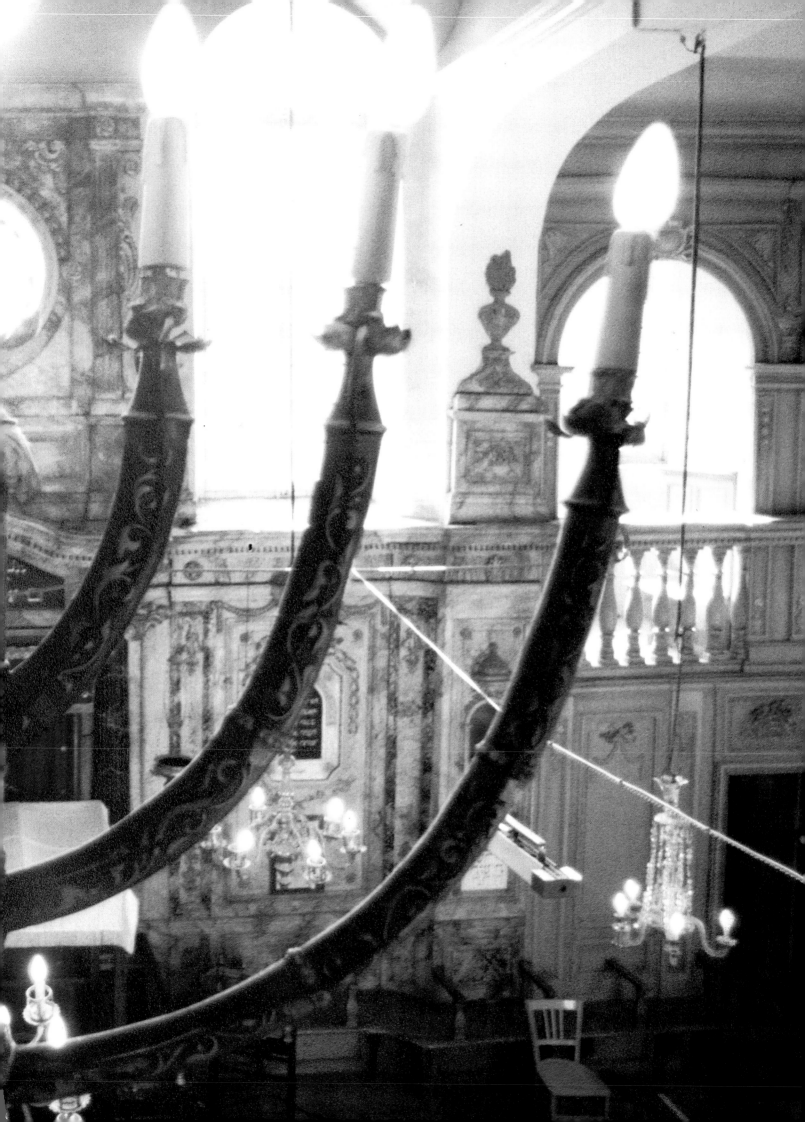

Just in front of the Ark is the *bimah*, the dais for the reader of the *Torah* and the prayer. The *bimah* is more centrally positioned than the Aron. The congregation sit on chairs or benches on either side of the *bimah*, in front of the Ark.

A woman's position in the synagogue is influenced by the sociological context, and differs from one community to another, according to the degree of orthodoxy. Traditionally, women are placed behind the men, separated by a *me'hitsa*, an object which acts as a divider, whether a curtain, a gate, a grating, a folding screen, or a sliding door. Women are often positioned one floor above the men, grouped in a semi-circular fashion, overlooking the men and essentially with a view of the Ark and the *bima*.

Today, given the growing number of protests by women (justified, in our opinion) over their participation in synagogue rituals, certain communities have placed the *me'hitsa* in the centre of the ground floor, with men on the left and women on the right. Other more reformed communities allow women to sit where they like, and they are given the same liturgical rights as men.

II. THE *MINYAN*

At least ten men thirteen years of age or older are necessary to form a *minyan*. This assembly is required for any communal prayer, whether the *Kaddish*, a reading from the *Torah*, or the *kiddusha* (given during the silent blessing given while one stands).

III. THE STRUCTURE OF PRAYER

Prayer was institutionalised after the des-

truction of the second Temple of Jerusalem. The Hebraic bible contains many examples of individual prayers, such as the one uttered by Moses for his sister, or that of Hannah, the mother of Samuel, to bear a child.

Communal prayer has replaced the offering of sacrifices to the Temple. During the week, three prayers are uttered each day: *shachris* in the morning; *mincha* in the afternoon, and *ma'ariv* in the evening. On the Sabbath and on holidays, another prayer, the *Musaf*, is added after the *shachris*.

All prayers are found in the book of prayers called the *Siddur*. Special prayers for certain days, *Yom Kippur* for example, are found in a special *Siddur* called the *Mahzor*, which contains prayers and biblical passages to be read on that day. Thus, the prayers of *Yom Kippur* are found in the *Mahzor* of *Yom Kippur*.

The structure of the prayer is essentially the same for all communities, but sometimes the order or the importance of certain passages to be read differs, according to custom.

All Jews pray facing east, in the direction of Jerusalem and the vestiges of its Temple.

(1) House of Study (cf. chapter 20)

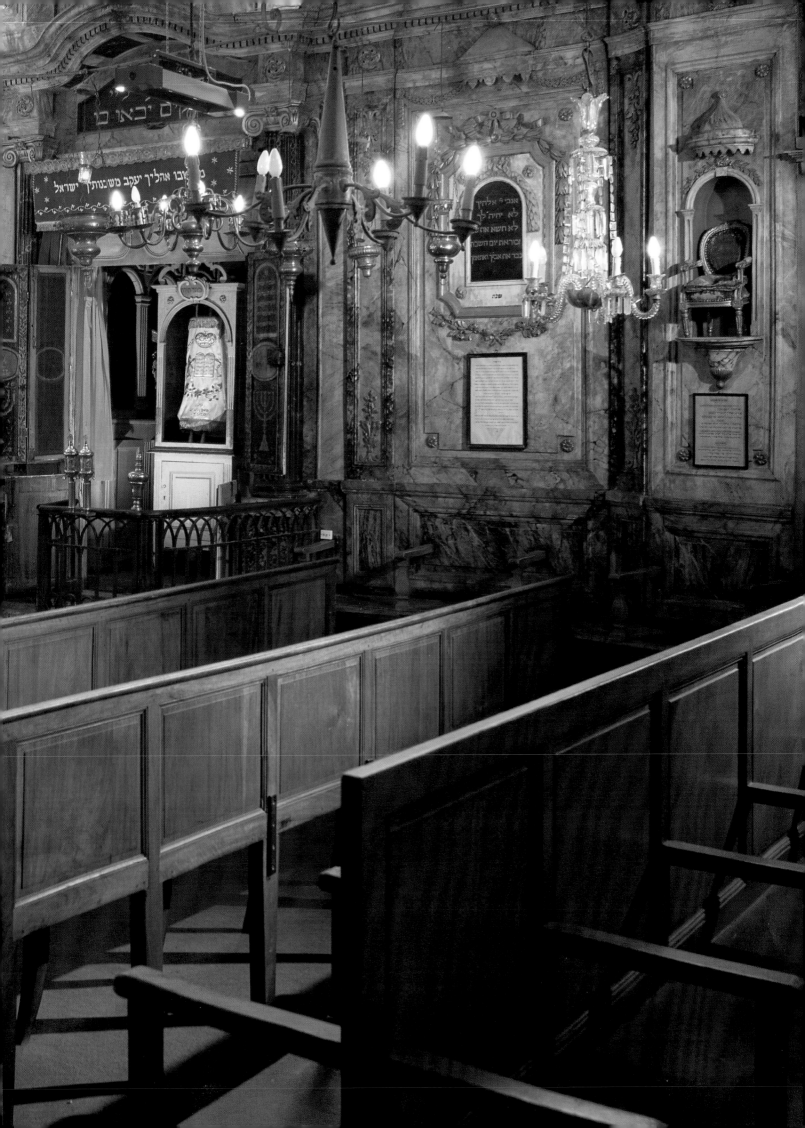

CHAPTER 7

THE SEFER TORAH

THE HANDWRITTEN PARCHMENT
SCROLL CONTAINING THE FIVE BOOKS OF MOSES
IN THE *TORAH* IS USED FOR PUBLIC
READINGS IN THE SYNAGOGUE.

THE MAKING OF THE SCROLLS, THE DISTINCTIVE STYLE OF THE HANDWRITING, THE PAGE DESIGN, AND THEIR DECORATIVE DETAILS ARE fascinating from both an intellectual and artistic point of view. One of the most important liturgical acts in the synagogue is the reading from the *Torah*, the Five Books of Moses:

– Genesis: *Bereshith;*

– Exodus: *Shemoth;*

– Leviticus: *Va-yikra;*

– Numbers: *Bamidbar;*

– Deuteronomy: *Devorim;*

The tradition of reading the *Torah* in public three times a week began during the epoch of Ezra, in the sixth century of the pre-common era. It is read on Mondays, Thursdays and Saturdays, as well as on holidays, *Rosh Hodesh* (the first day of every month), and days of fasting. At least ten people (a *minyan*) must be gathered in order to perform the public reading.

Three to seven people are called upon to read a passage or say a blessing before the reading, which usually is given by specialists of biblical cantillation. The entire *Torah* is read over a period of a year. It is divided into fifty-four parts, each called *sedra*, which means order, or *parashah*, which means "piece" or "passage". Every Sabbath, a different part is read.

The cycle begins on the Sabbath following the festival of *Simhath Torah*, which brings the autumn holidays to a close; the cycle ends on *Simhath Torah* of the following year.

Thus, from week to week, on each Saturday, biblical history accompanies the Jewish people, from the creation of the world to the death of Moses and the entrance into the "Promised Land". Jews throughout the world read the same text on the same day.

The name of each of the fifty-four sections is taken from the first word, or one of the first words, of each of the verses of the *parashah*. In this manner, the first *parashah* is called *Bereshith* — the first word of the first verse of the *Torah*. The Sabbath also adopts the name of the *parashah*. For example, *Bereshith* Sabbath is when the passage concerning *Bereshith* is read.

During the public service, after the blessings, the Psalms, the *Shema Yisrael* and the *Amidah* (the silent prayer said while standing with both feet together) have all been read, the Scrolls of the Law, or the *Sifrei Torah* (plural of *Sefer Torah*), are taken out of the Ark. These are kept at one end of the synagogue, facing the entranceway, and turned towards Jerusalem.

The location of the Ark is determined by its relative position to Jerusalem.

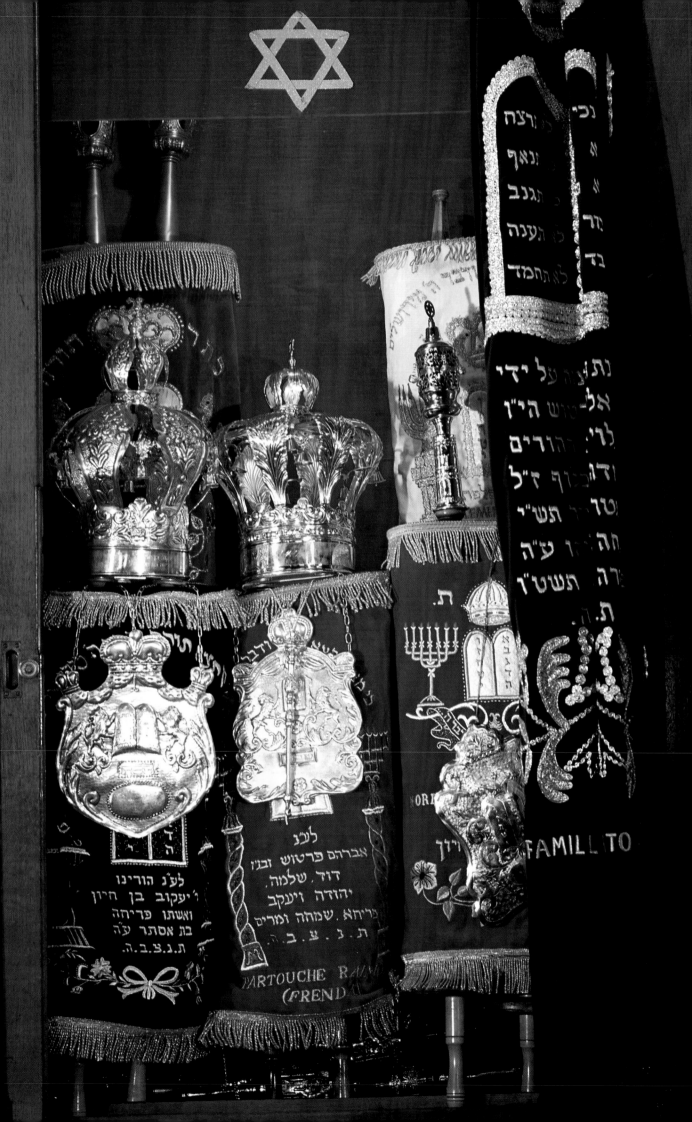

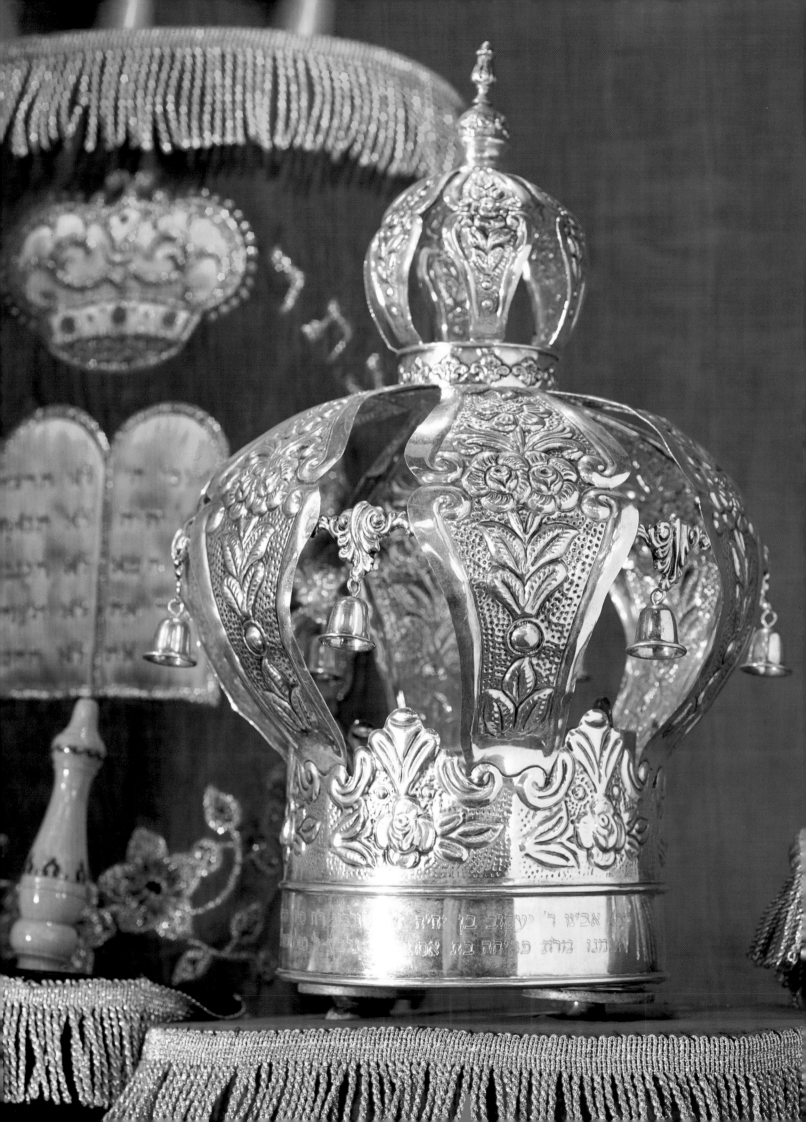

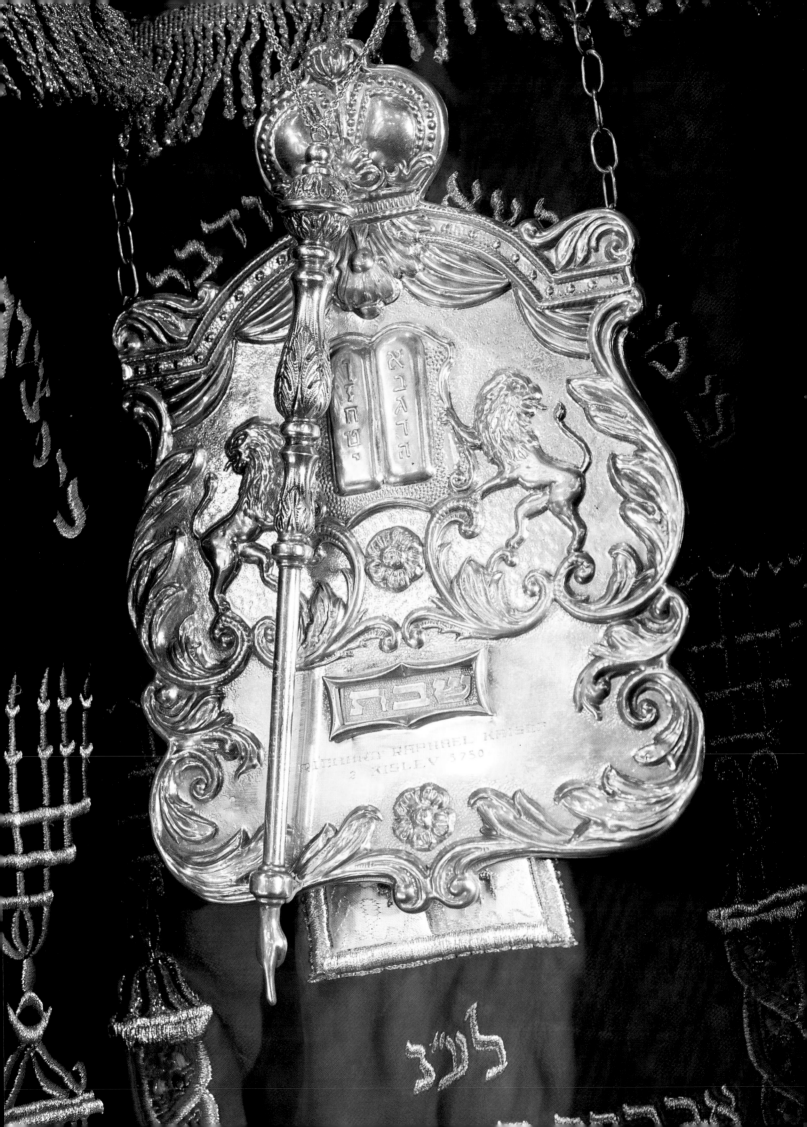

THE HOLY ARK OR THE ARON HAKODESH. The Ark is a chest or receptacle which usually contains several scrolls wrapped in mantles richly adorned and embroidered with gold or silver threads on which the names of donors are sewn, and the name of the occasion for which they have been donated.

THE ADORNMENTS. Silver plates (or plates of other kinds of metal) are attached to the mantles and bear smaller detachable plates engraved with the name of the *parashah* of the week. The ends of the wooden holders on which the scrolls are mounted bear one or two tiny crowns called *Rimmonim* (literally, pomegranates).

THE POINTER OR THE YAD. A finger or hand made of silver, wood or any other material assists the handling of the text during the reading, as touching the scrolls with bare hands is forbidden.

THE *HAGBAHAH* OR THE EXHIBITION OF THE *TORAH*. A member of the congregation is called upon to open the Ark and to carry the scrolls from the Ark to the reading table in the centre of the synagogue. The table is called the *tevah* or the *bimah*. Each scroll is then placed on the table and "undressed" as its outer adornments are removed.

The scrolls are opened up to the passage to be read, for they will be shown to the assembly. A member of the congregation comes forward to raise the open scroll and show it to all others present in the congregation.

To do this, he turns around, raising his arms up high. This public presentation is called the *Hagbahah* , meaning "to rise up".

It is a great honour to be chosen to perform the *Hagbahah* , to read or recite a blessing aloud before the open scrolls. For special occasions, there is open bidding to determine who will perform these different ceremonies. This is an indirect way of having congregation members donate funds for the upkeep of the synagogue. It is also customary to give a donation when going up to the *Torah*. (1)

TOOLS OF THE SCRIBE. The books of the *Torah* or of the *Sifrei Torah* are on scrolls made from parched or tanned leather. The scrolls are formed by sewing strips of skin together. The sacred texts are copied onto the scrolls using a calamus reed in the East, and a goose quill in the West.

The scribe or *Sofer* writes by hand following a model to avoid mistakes. He uses a special ink which is not easily erased, and is very durable.

THE STRUCTURE OF THE *TORAH* TEXT. The text uses no vowels. Only consonants form words, which make the reading difficult, and demands much preparation to learn how to read and cantillate it properly. There is no punctuation, so nothing indicates the rhythm or the transition from one sentence to the next. Nothing breaks up the flow of these words, except blank spaces, or writing voids, which appear to the untrained eye as gaps in the middle of the writing. The text between two blank spaces is called *parashah*, or

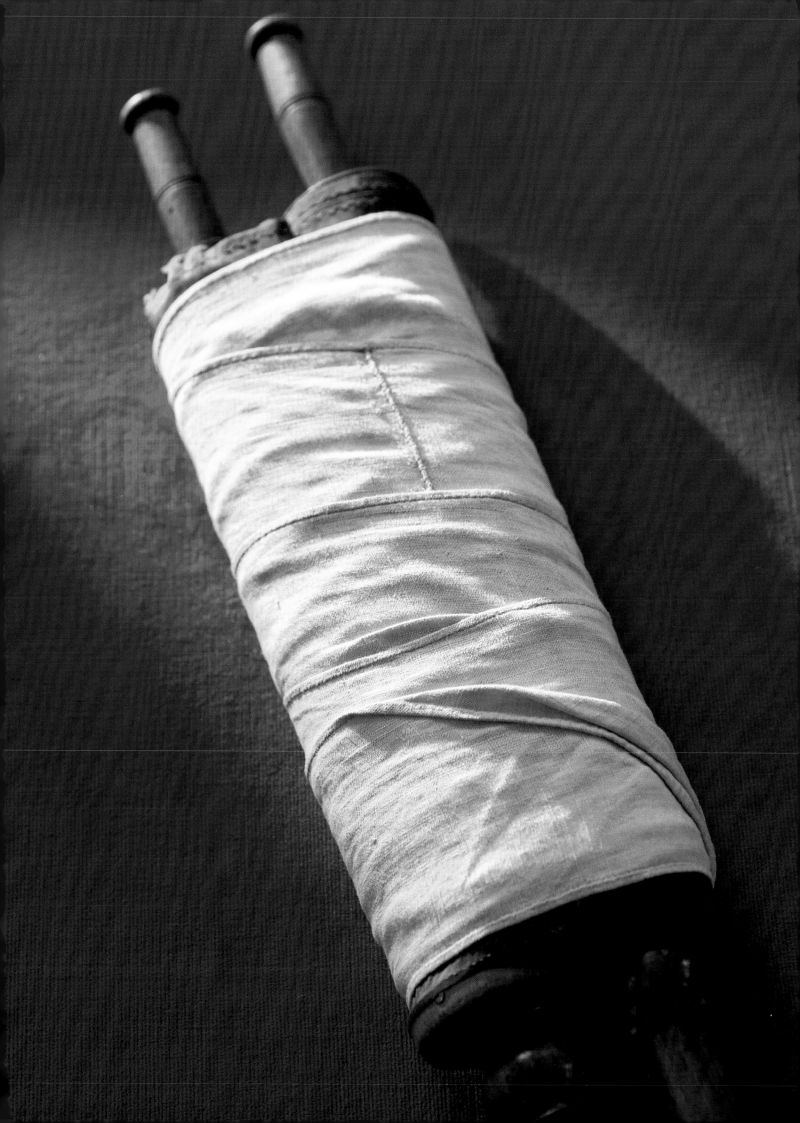

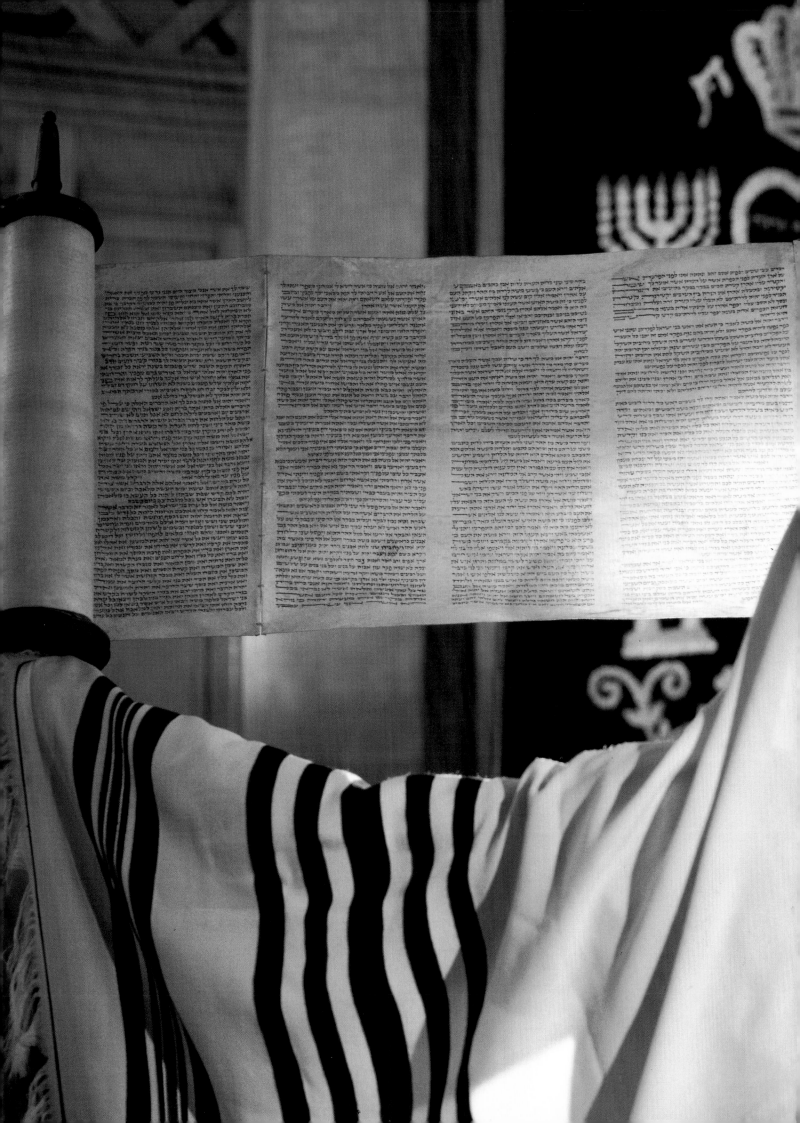

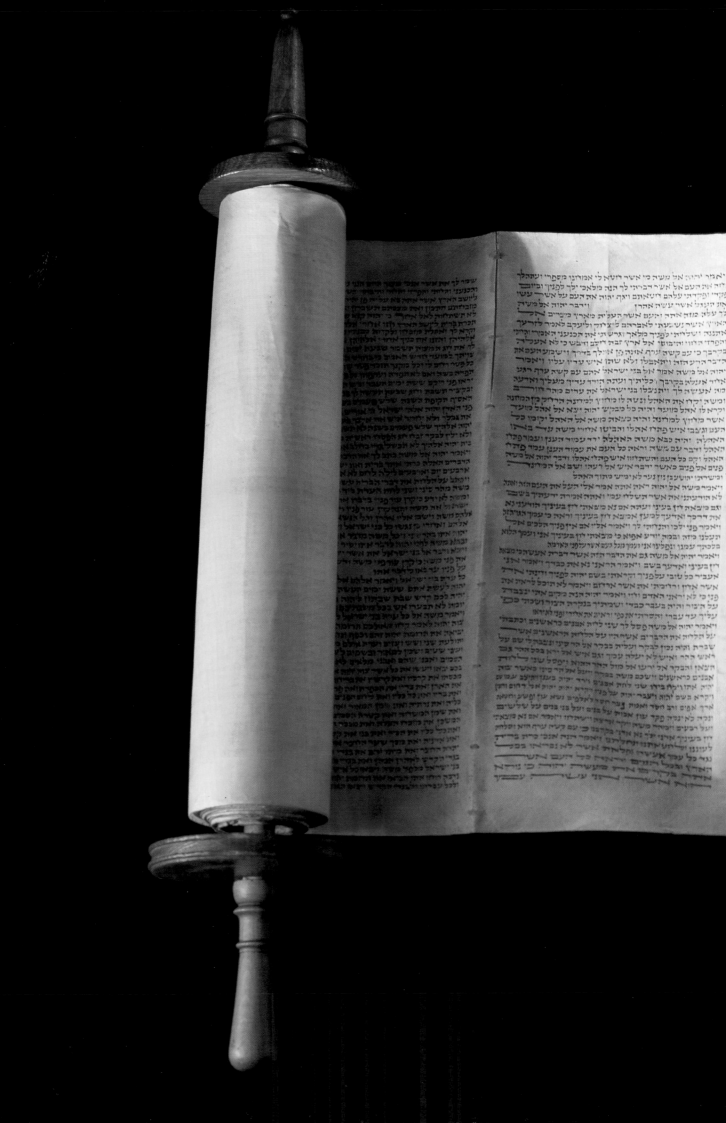

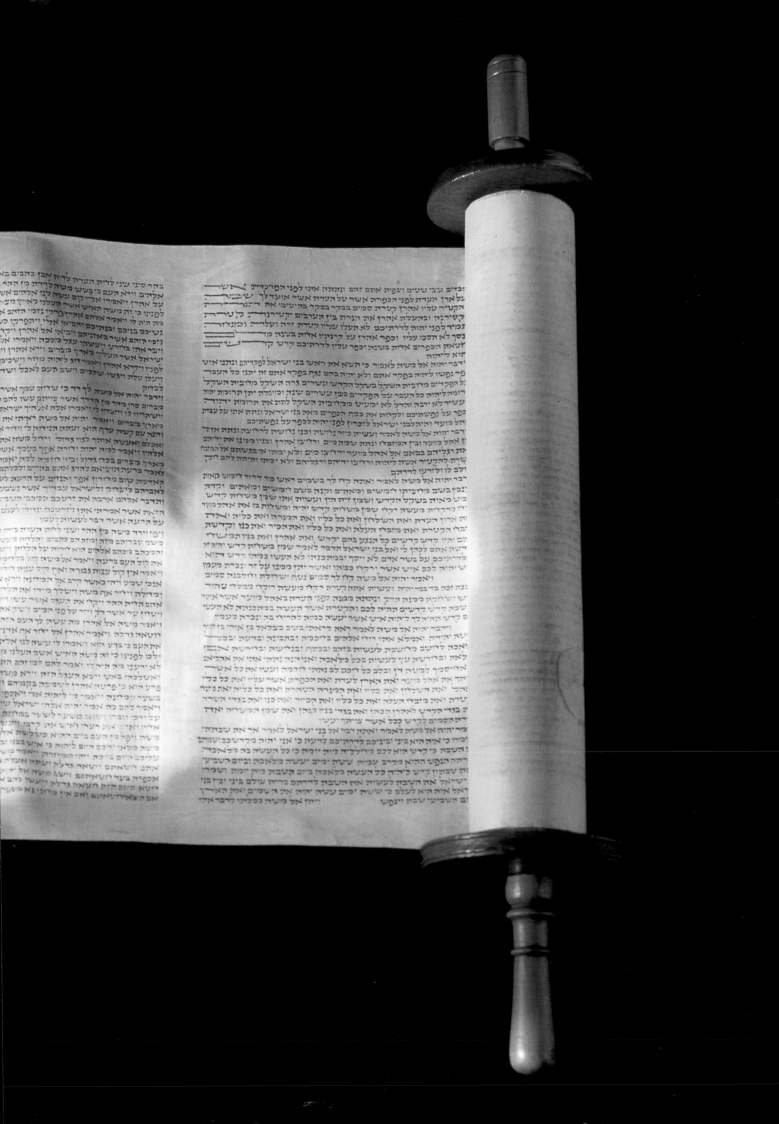

"passage". The books of the *Torah* are separated by a space of four lines.

Certain letters are topped with small flourishes, called crowns. More specifically, the left side of seven of the twenty-two letters in the Hebrew alphabet are decorated with three small strokes or crowns. These seven letters are: *shin, teth, nun, zayin, gimel,* and *sadhe.*

To fully grasp the meaning of the crowns, another comment should be added: as Rabbi Tsadoq Hakohen of Lublin has pointed out, there is an essential difference in writing Hebrew and Latin letters. It concerns the positioning of the letter in relation to the "base line". In Latin, the letter sits on a line below it. In Hebrew, however, the letter is suspended from, or hangs below, the line. For example:

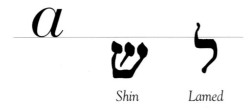

Shin   Lamed

The top line represents a barrier. It has a symbolic meaning because it delineates the boundary between the writing and that which exists beyond the writing. None of the twenty-two letters of the Hebrew alphabet goes beyond this limit, with one exception.

The name of the letter in question encloses its meaning in its form. *Lamed* is the semantic root of all things related to study and teaching — teaching that literally follows the directive of this letter, lamed, which says "to learn it". To learn is to enter into the movement of going beyond the boundary line of the writing, to go "beyond" the text. *Lamed* which means "to learn". The word *Talmud,* the seminal book of Jewish thought, is derived from this letter. The *Talmud* does not represent a collection of inherited knowledge, but an exacting pursuit of research, questioning and interpretation. Writing a book is one of the 613 commandments. There is thus a tradition of writing a book, or having a book or part of a book written in one's own name.

Some communities pool their resources to buy a book of the Torah, with each member buying a letter, a chapter or an entire passage.

If copies of the *Sefer Torah,* prayer books, *mezuzot* or *tefillin* are worn or damaged, they are not destroyed. They are buried in a section of the Jewish cemetery, or grouped together in the *genizah,* which is an area usually in a room of the synagogue, or near the synagogue.

The *genizah* in Cairo which was discovered at the end of the nineteenth century has proved invaluable to historical research. It contained ancient manuscripts of many sacred texts, as well as precious details about daily life, commerce, customs and voyages of many Jews over an extended period of time.

(1) According to the Sephardic tradition, the *Hagbahah* is done before the reading of the *Torah,* but in the Ashkenasic tradition the *Hagbahah* takes place after the reading.

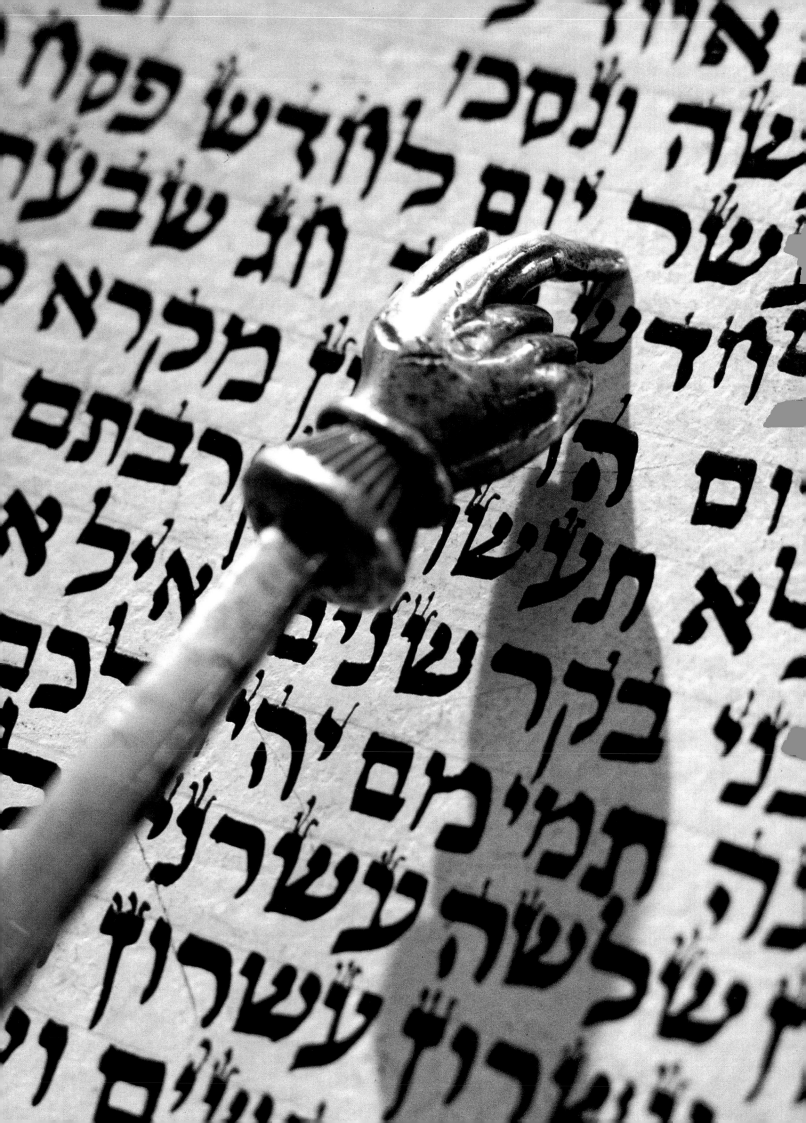

CHAPTER 8

THE SABBATH

THE SABBATH IS ONE OF THE MOST IMPORTANT
EVENTS IN THE JEWISH RELIGION. IT IS OBSERVED AS
A HOLY DAY AND A PUBLIC HOLIDAY.

IN THE HEBREW BIBLE, THE SABBATH IS THE SEVENTH DAY OF CREATION, AND IT IS THE DAY OF REST. THE WORD SABBATH IN HEBREW means to rest from all creative activity. It is a day of rest for the entire Jewish household, whether master, slave, animal or visitor.

The commandment for observing the Sabbath is the fourth commandment of the Decalogue, which states that Jews must observe this holy day in memory of the Exodus from Egypt.

The fourth commandment is also a reminder that God created the world in six days and rested on the seventh, and this is why he blessed the day of the Sabbath and made it holy. Although work is not permitted on the seventh day, there are certain duties to be accomplished.

The activities forbidden during the Sabbath are listed in the thirty-nine classes of prohibited work. The activities which must be performed revolve around the *eruv*, the *nerot*, the *Kiddush*, the *challah*, the reading of the *Torah*, the *seudah*, and the *Havdalah*. These terms will be explored in this chapter.

I. THE THIRTY-NINE CLASSES OF PROHIBITED WORK.

Those forbidden on the Sabbath. According to the *Talmud*, the origin of these classes is found in the interpretation of the following verse: "You will build my sanctuary, yet you will respect my Sabbath".

It is understood by this that all labours involved in building the Temple are forbidden on the Sabbath. As the philosopher A.Y. Heschel argued in his book with the very apt title *The Builders of Time*, it is a question of man leaving the dimension of space and technique to enter the inner dimension of time. These thirty-nine labours cover a panoply of creative acts.

The basic activities are: 1. sowing; 2. ploughing; 3. reaping; 4. binding sheaves; 5. threshing; 6. winnowing; 7. cleansing (crops); 8. grinding; 9. sifting; 10. kneading; 11. baking; 12. shearing (wool); 13. washing (wool); 14. beating (wool); 15. dyeing; 16. spinning; 17. weaving; 18. looping; 19. warping; 20. unwarping; 21. tying a knot; 22. loosening (a knot); 23. stitching; 24. tearing;

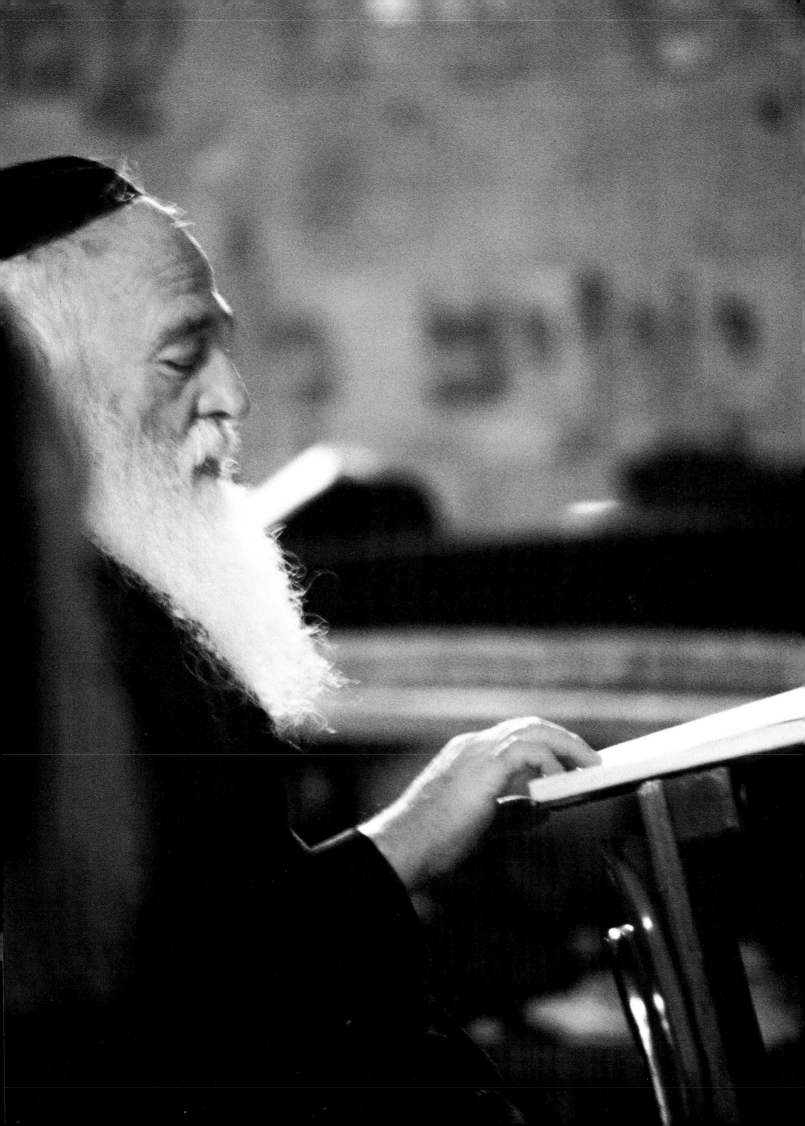

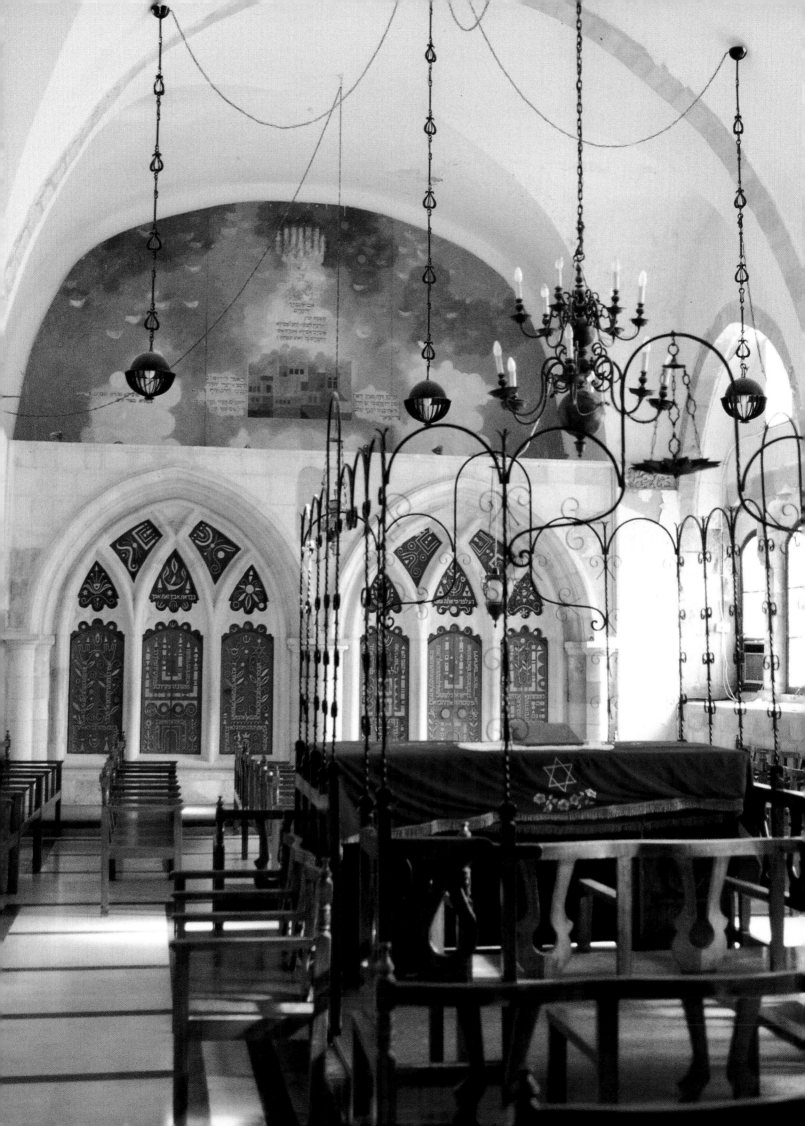

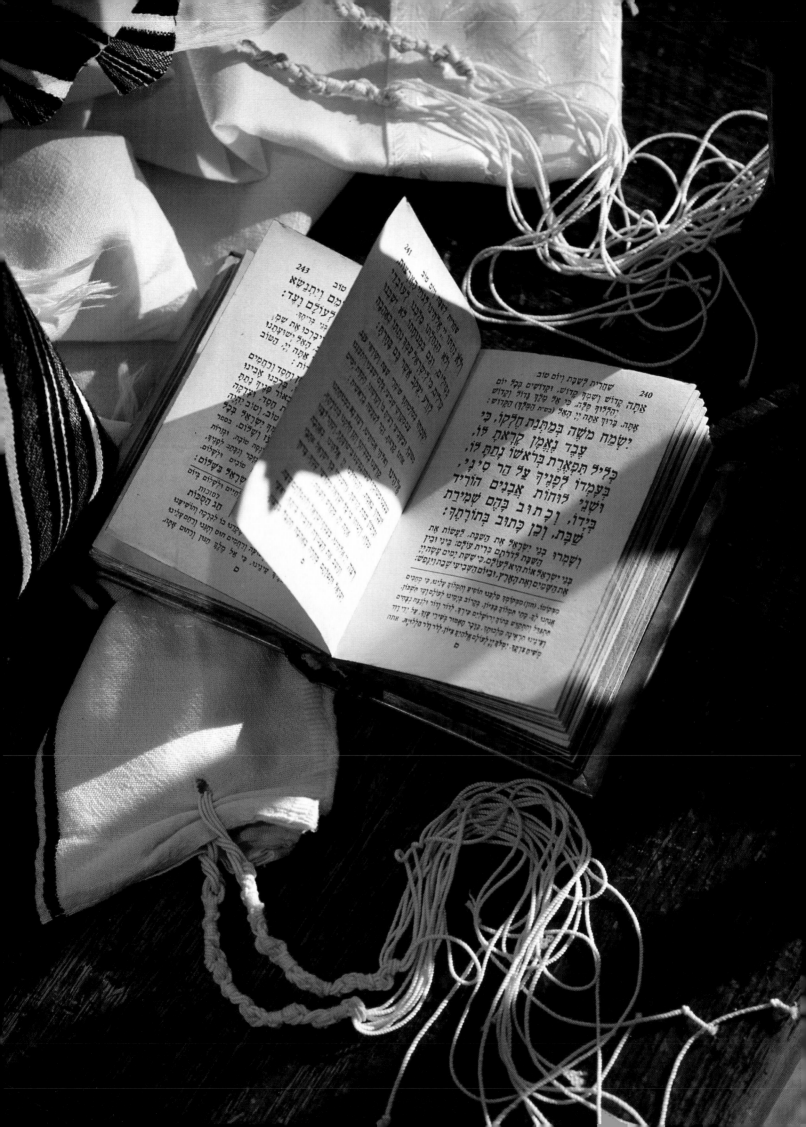

25. hunting; 26. slaughtering; 27. flaying; 28. salting; 29. tanning; 30. scraping (a skin); 31. cutting up (a skin); 32. writing; 33. erasing; 34. building; 35. breaking; 36. extinguishing a fire; 37. kindling a fire; 38. striking with a hammer; 39. carrying from one place to another (1).

To this rather lengthy list, the ancients added bans on related labours: it is also forbidden to cook any food on the Sabbath, which is an extension of the ban on baking bread. Many objects must be cast aside before the Sabbath, such as pencils and other writing utensils, or matches for lighting fires, as these objects could easily be picked up and used inadvertently. These additional prohibitions are seen as barriers that reinforce the observing of the Sabbath. It must be noted, however, that they are all instantly annulled if they are involved in saving someone's life, or a person is in serious danger.

Although these restrictions would appear to impinge on one's freedom, they actually permit man to devote effort and energy to activities of a different nature. During the week, man invests space; during the Sabbath, he invests time. During the week, man's energies are spent with objects; during the Sabbath, his energies are spent on time. The Sabbath is dedicated to rest, but also to study, conversation, walks, and visiting friends. In philosophical terms, putting a distance between object and person allows for self-improvement: improvement of the person in relation to himself and to those around him. All the rituals of the Sabbath highlight this social dimension of conviviality and meeting with others.

II. THE NEROT:
THE FRIDAY NIGHT CANDLES

The beginning of the Sabbath is marked by the ritual lighting of two candles. Everything must be ready by the time the Sabbath begins. The house should be cleaned, the meals cooked, the table set, baths taken, and everyone in the family dressed for celebration. Sabbath begins an hour before nightfall on Friday and ends at sunset on Saturday. It lasts twenty-five hours in all.

Two or more candles, or *nerot*, are placed in candlesticks. Candelabra feature prominently in traditional Jewish art, and some of the most beautiful examples can be found finely crafted out of filigree silver. In every Jewish household, the candelabrum is a basic symbol of attachment to traditional values.

Today, despite assimilation, it still holds a respected place in the home, even if celebration of the Sabbath is only a memory associated with parents or grandparents. The lighting of these candles marks the beginning of Sabbath. It is usually the woman of the house who gives the blessing as she lights each *ner*. The Kabbalists say that the light from the Sabbath candles repairs the damage done by the first man on earth. It erases the darkness brought by original sin. After the candles have been lit, everyone goes to the synagogue to take part in the Friday night service, which differs from those of the other evenings of the week.

Once back in the home, several more canticles are sung, and then it is customary for the father and the mother to bless their children by

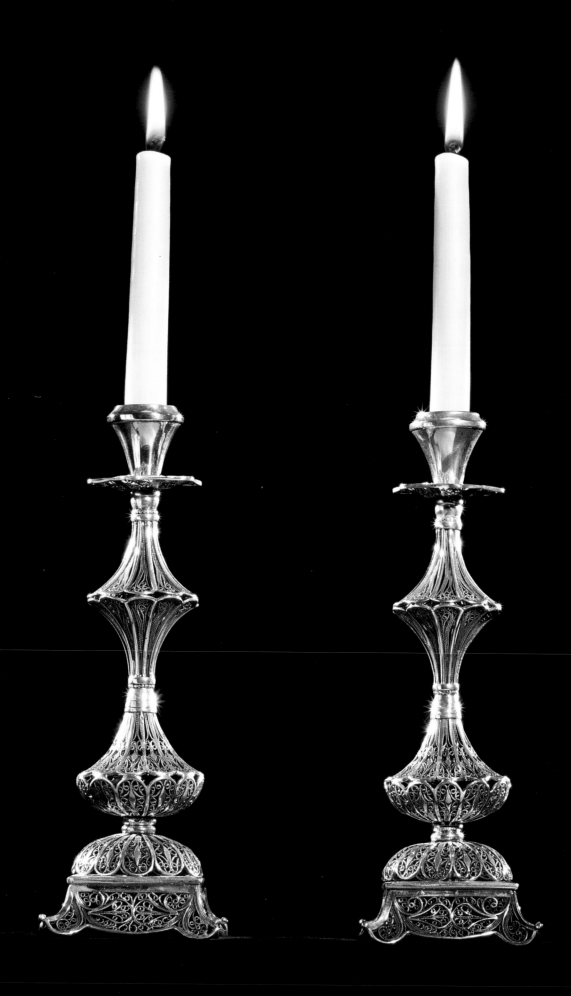

placing two hands on their head and reciting a few verses of the *Torah*.

III. THE *KIDDUSH*: THE GOBLET OF WINE

The Sabbath and holy days are times for people to meet with God, and with others. This meeting, or *moed*, is considered a sacred time. The sanctification of time in the Jewish tradition is always marked by a blessing given over wine.

The *Kiddush*, which literally means sanctification, is a ceremony where a blessing is given over a goblet of wine. Time is sanctified through this blessing, symbolised by the goblet of wine. This blessing inaugurates many festive meals, in this case, the first meal of the Sabbath.

The blessing is a reminder that the Sabbath marks the creation of the world, that God created the world in six days, and ceased all creative activity to rest on the seventh. This is why man must stop working on this day. It is also mentioned that the Sabbath is kept in remembrance of the exodus from Egypt and of the wandering through the desert. The Kabbalists point out that the Hebrew word for goblet or glass (of wine), *Kosse*, has a numerical value of 86, which is the same as that of the God *Elohim*.

Kabbalist texts explain that wine has a numerical value of 70, the same numerical value as the word *Sod*, meaning "secret". Numerous speculations are based on these games of numbers and letters, allowing the ritual to be structured by writing the language onto objects. According to the same Kabbalistic tradition, the *Kiddush* glass should be raised with two hands.

IV. CHALLAH: THE SABBATH BREAD

After the *Kiddush*, the hands are washed (*Netilat Yadayim*) in a special recipient, the *Keli*, then a blessing is given over the *challah* loaves, which are covered with a napkin or cloth often richly decorated. The Sabbath meal begins with the blessing of the Sabbath — two braided loaves of bread which symbolise the two portions of manna (2) which fell from the sky onto the desert on Friday. This bread is specially made for the Sabbath, each woman having her own recipe.

It is interesting to note that manna is one of the underlying themes of Judaism. After the cries of hunger and thirst from the children of Israel reached the ears of Moses, God let a small white grain rain down on the desert, a grain which looked like coriander seed, and which no man had ever seen before.

As they came out of their tents on the morning after the manna had dropped, each person asked of his neighbour, "What is it?" And Moses answered: "It is bread from the sky, sent to you by God!" And God then told them, "Because you have said 'what is it?,' the name of the bread will be 'what is it?'" (3). And for forty years, the children of Israel ate "What is it?" It is the fundamental experience of questioning which opens man to both searching and adventure.

By beginning the Sabbath with the blessing of the *challah*, one enters the time of the Sabbath via a question, via the questioning of oneself, making the necessary renewal of the self possible.

It has been pointed out several times in this chapter that the Sabbath is a day of rest. A state

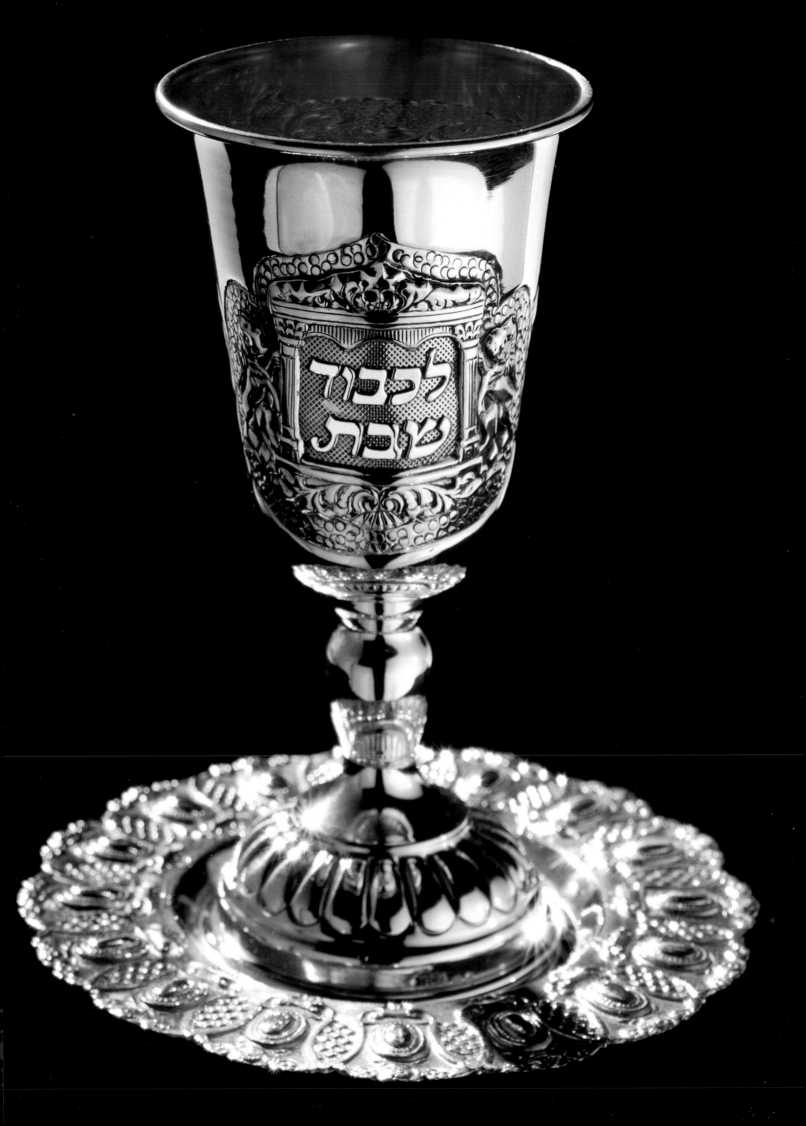

of emptiness is entered into, not so that the void be filled, but to avoid a life which is too full, which could overwhelm us.

The question raised by the manna provides us with an opportunity to construct time. The expression literally translated as "Here is the Manna" in Hebrew, means "time".

During the meal, the Sabbath songs or *Zemiroth* are sung, and the meal ends with the final blessing *Birchat Ha-mazon*.

V. THE READING OF THE *TORAH* DURING THE MORNING SERVICE OF THE SABBATH

One of the important moments of the Sabbath is the liturgical reading of the *Torah* during the morning service of the Sabbath. The Saturday morning service at the synagogue begins with the morning prayer, and is followed by the reading of a passage of the Torah. Every Sabbath section or *parashah* is subdivided into seven parts, and for each one of them a person is called up to assist in the reading. A passage from the Prophets is then read, chosen according to the section of the week, the *Haftarah*. The reading is followed by an additional Sabbath prayer, the *Musaf*, which is the additional service closing the morning service.

VI. THE *SEUDAH*

The Sabbath is a time for socialising, for meeting up with friends and acquaintances. This is generally spent sharing meals, where songs are sung and passages of the *Torah* read during the Sabbath are discussed.

Usually, a *seudah* or meal is served three times during the Sabbath. A blessing is made over two loaves of bread at the beginning of the first meal, and at the end the *Birchat Ha-Mazone*, the blessing of food is recited. The first *seudah* takes place on Friday night. The second *seudah* begins after the morning Sabbath service.

The meal begins with the *Kiddush*, followed by the blessing over the two loaves of bread, as on Friday night.

The third meal, or *seudah sh'leeshith* is served after the afternoon service, just before the Sabbath draws to a close. During this meal, melancholic songs are sung, for it is with a certain sadness that one prepares to leave behind the special and holy feeling of the Sabbath.

VII. THE *HAVDALAH*: THE CLOSING CERE-MONY OF THE SABBATH

The Sabbath is brought to a close with a separation ritual. The ceremony is very poetic, and the objects used are highly symbolic, which has made the ritual a source of inspiration for artists. In the dancing shadows from the flickering light thrown by the flame of a twisted candle, a blessing is given over the wine, then over the perfume, over light and, lastly, over the separation between the holy time of the Sabbath, and the secular time of the other days of the week.

The word *Havdalah* means separation, that of the Sabbath from that which follows the Sabbath. At nightfall on Saturday, a final ceremony is performed, with the first blessing given over the wine, then another blessing over a perfumed plant,

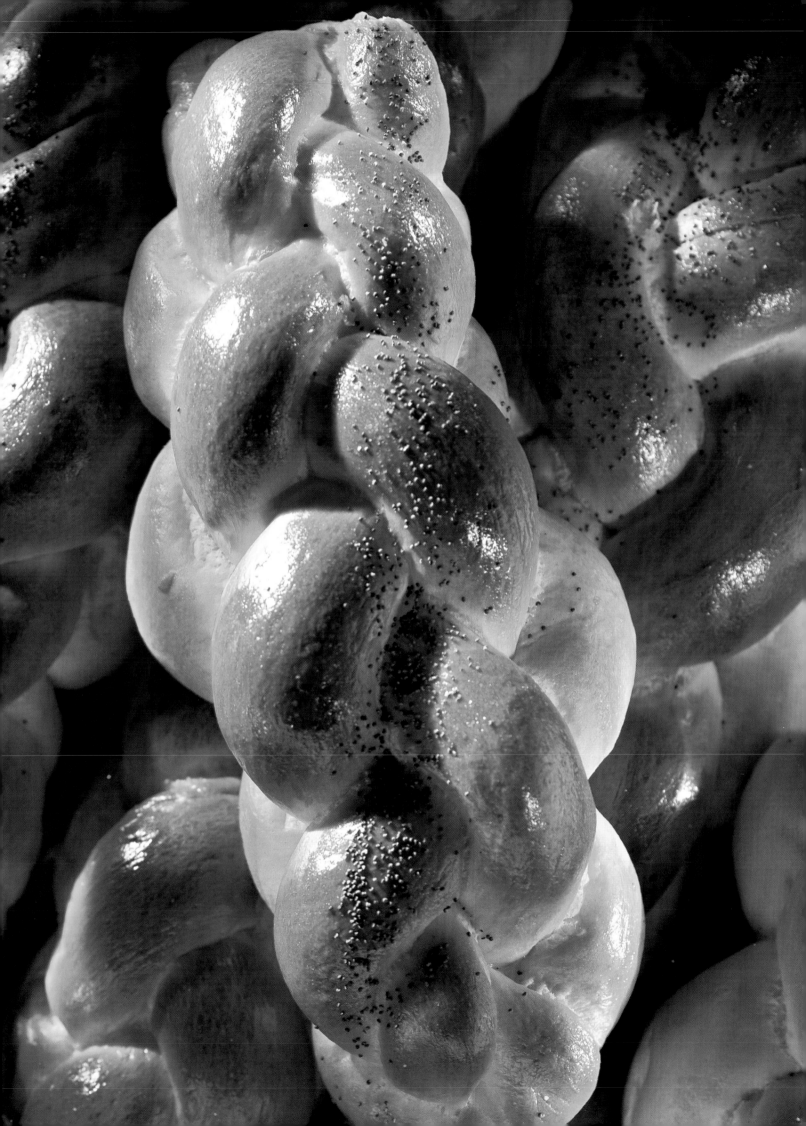

which represents the good smells of the Sabbath, and the last blessing over the flame.

In its shadow, the fingernails are contemplated to pay homage to the transparence of the first man in contrast to our opaque nature. At the end of the ceremony, a few drops of wine are poured over the flame to extinguish it. *Havdalah* wine is not passed out to all who have assisted, as it is in the *Kiddush*. Instead, it is drunk only by the person who read the *Havdalah*. These days, it is customary to make wishes for the coming week.

The *Havdalah* brings an end to all the restrictions imposed by the Sabbath. Beautifully-crafted and highly valuable examples of the objects used in this ceremony have been produced over the years, namely, of the *Besamim* (spice box) and the *Havdalah* twisted candlestick holders. The most original object of the ceremony is the spice box, which, in Germany and Eastern European countries, is known as *Gewürzbüchse* or *Bessomim-büchse*. Boxes shaped like turrets are the most common, but others can be shaped like fruit such as apples or pears.

There are also boxes in the form of flowers, eggs, acorns, fish, and sometimes, steam engines. In fact, there is a great variety of shapes, ranging from swans to roosters, and from windmills to horse-drawn coaches.

They are generally made out of solid or filigree silver. For the *Havdalah* ceremony, the boxes are filled with cloves or myrtle leaves.

What does the perfume ritual mean? Why is the perfume from plants inhaled as the Sabbath draws to a close? According to Kabbalistic communities, man receives an additional soul the evening before the Sabbath.

This soul releases its pungency during the Sabbath, and returns into the world of souls at the end of the Sabbath. Man, feeling this loss, falls into nostalgia, and uses the perfume as a slight "lift".

(1) It is forbidden to carry anything from a private to a public place over a distance of more than four lengths of an elbow (about two steps).
However, if an area, even an entire city, is surrounded by a rope or line linking posts that are at least forty centimetres high, then this may be considered an enclosed single space, and objects may be carried in it during the Sabbath. This line is called the *eruv*.
(2) During the long period of living in the desert, the Hebrews ate manna and quail which fell miraculously from the sky. However, biblical text states that two loaves of bread need to be collected on Friday, as no manna fell on the Sabbath.
(3) In Hebrew: "Mannehou".

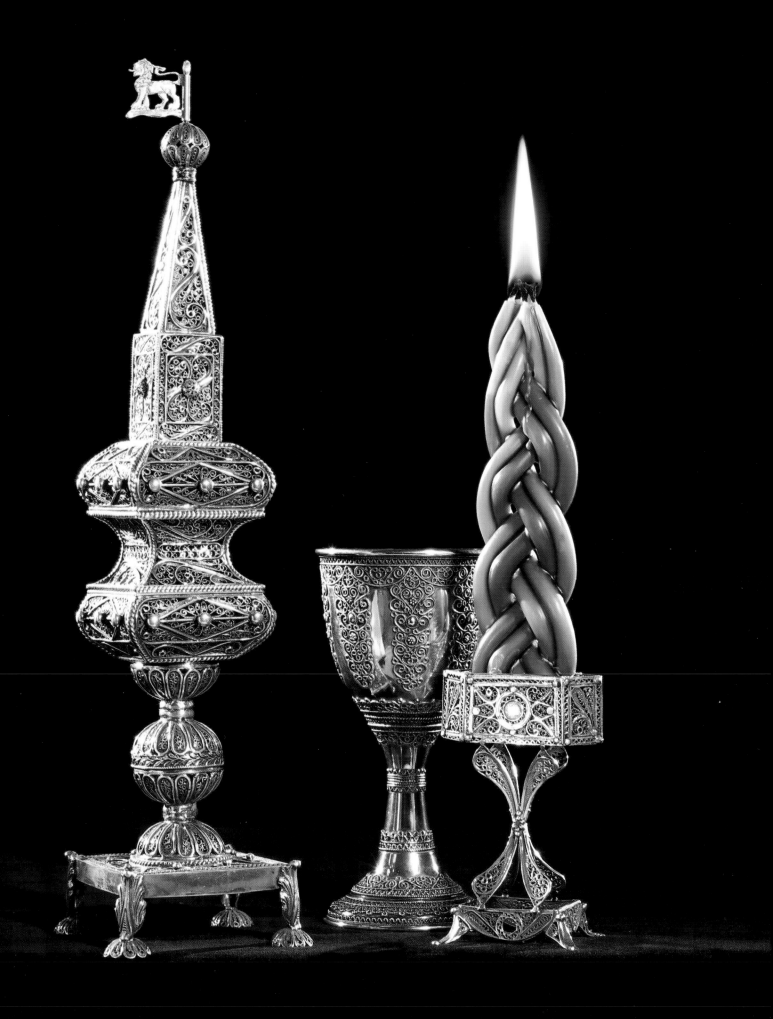

CHAPTER 9

THE SHOFAR

THE *SHOFAR* IS A RAM'S HORN USED
AS A MUSICAL INSTRUMENT ON THE DAYS OF *ROSH
HASHANAH*, THE JEWISH NEW YEAR, AND AFTER
YOM KIPPUR, THE DAY OF ATONEMENT.

WHEN ABRAHAM WAS OFFERING HIS SON ISAAC IN SACRIFICE ON DIVINE ORDER, AN ANGEL INTERVENED, PREVENTING THE murder by choosing a ram to be sacrificed instead.

What was called the sacrifice of Isaac became known as "the non-sacrifice of Isaac", which changed the course of man's thinking. Human sacrifice would no longer be committed from this moment onwards. A ram's horn is blown during certain Jewish ceremonies to pay respect to this animal which saved Isaac's life. Symbolically, the gesture means that if a human must die, the same miracle should occur for him. The *shofar* holds a privileged place at the heart of *Rosh Hashanahh* and *Yom Kippur* festivities, days of judgment and pardon.

Three different patterns of notes are sounded on the *shofar*. The first is long and sustained, called *tekiah*, which means "to be fixed, driven into the ground".

The second pattern is made up of three notes of equal length, each one-third of the length of a *tekiah*. This pattern is called *shebarim*, which means "broken" notes.

The third category is made up of nine short series of notes, all equal in length, all one-ninth of a *tekiah* or one-third of a *shebarim*. This pattern is called *teruah* and means "shaking into motion".

When each of these patterns of notes has been played, the sequence is closed with a repeat of the *tekiah* (the long unbroken pattern of notes).

Téquia ——————————————————

Chévarim ————— ————— —————

Téroua — — — — — — — — —

Téquia ——————————————————

The rite of the *shofar* is symbolic of a certain definition of ethical man. The broken notes of the *shebarim* are there as a reminder that man can escape from imprisonment within a closed definition of himself.

This is what shapes his freedom, which distinguishes him as being separate from manufactured objects and animals. Objects are defined things, while man is undefined. He is not identifiable or representable. He bears the pattern of broken notes, and refuses to qualify his essence, to enclose himself in any historical or natural definition. In Hebrew, the word which means "I" also means "nothingness". According to the *zohar*, this is to teach man the ability and his duty to not give a concrete definition of his essence. The *zohar* goes even further, emphasising the numeric coincidence between the word *adam* (man) and *mah* (what? what is it?).

Man is fundamentally a *mah*, a questioning

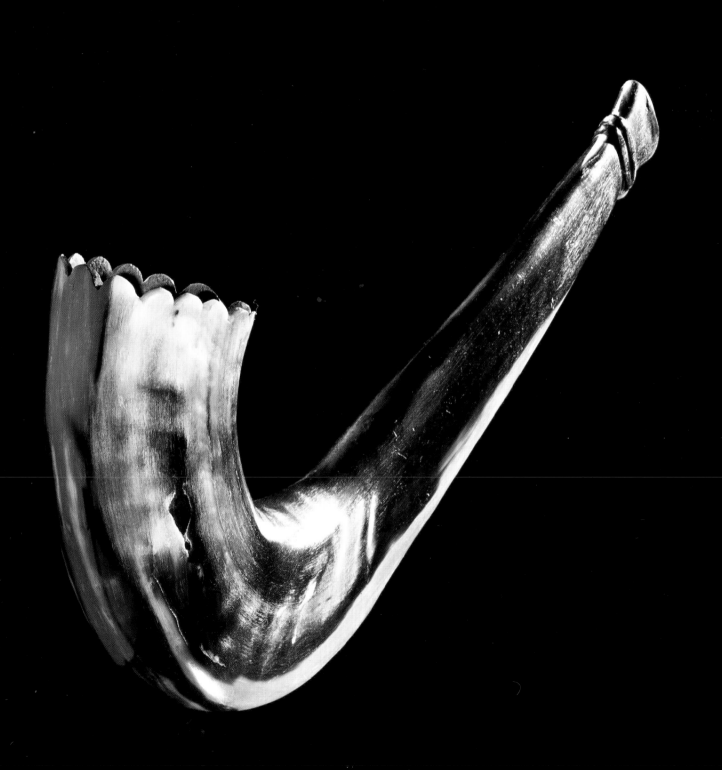

of himself, thus eliminating any risk of fixing himself with a definitive identity, whether it be natural or social. The "what-am-I-man" designates himself as a place of questioning, a process known in Hebrew as *Zeman*, "here is the question", and which signifies time. Human time, infinitive time, as opposed to definitive time.

Prohibition of representation or definition is sounded by the notes of the *shofar*. This prohibition does not concern the idol, but rather man himself. There are no idols, only idolaters. The banning of representation warns man against the neverending risk of merging with specific determinations of himself. It often happens that by accepting an imaginary representation of himself for a short period of time or permanently, the "what-am-I-man" becomes the "here's-the-man-that-I-am", identifying himself with a character or a role. This being done, he ceases to be part of the great "nothingness". In this reification, he loses a large part of his freedom. Having become the image he is resolved to adhere to, he abolishes distance, the nothingness, his internal difference, the engine of his evolution, and in so doing, he becomes an ethical being.

Returning to the musical patterns of the *shofar*, it could be asked, why are the *shebarim* followed by a *teruah*? Why should the interrupted sound be broken up a second time? This is because there is another derivative of definitive identity, that of a breaking up of identity, which also becomes a system. It is possible to come across beings who are happy with their "broken" image. But the breaking up mentioned earlier should be dynamic, dynamising. The *teruah* points out the need for a breaking up of what has already been broken, and the momentary reunion with the state of recomposing the "I", or the "me".

It is interesting to note that the word *shofar* also means the aesthetic aspect of things which are in a process of improving themselves, of embellishment. The Masters of the *Talmud* have always analysed the ethical embellishments in the way we define it: the continual transformation and change of human beings. The word *shofar* could also mean commentary, or interpretation — *perouch* (through a game of inter-changing letters around, the Hebrew language allows for multiple ways of reading the same word).

The dynamic of breaks, of breaking up the breaks, and of reunifying, fosters close bonds with the interpretation of texts and the world. The relationship of the ethical with interpretation is not just an experience of comprehending words and texts, but also a fundamental existentialist attitude that makes the reinventing of oneself possible.

To interpret, and study, is to interpret oneself....

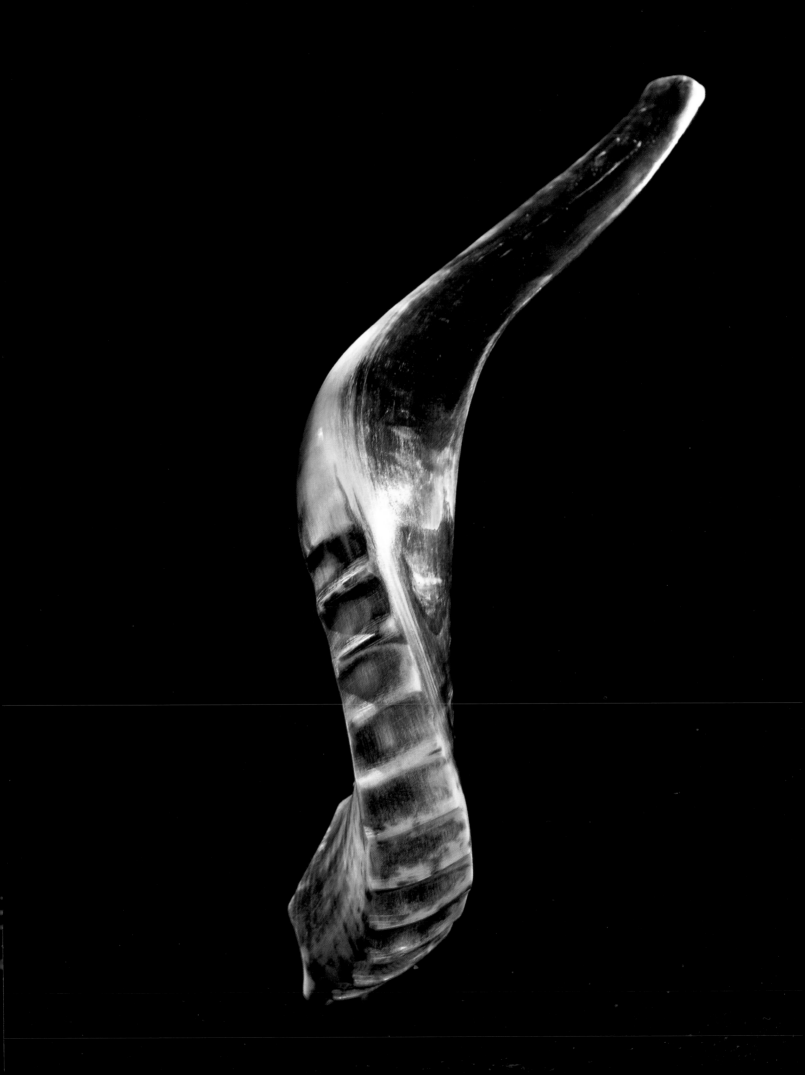

CHAPTER 10

ROSH HASHANAH

THE JEWISH NEW YEAR

ROSH HASHANAH, THE JEWISH NEW YEAR, IS A TWO-DAY HOLIDAY WHICH FALLS ON THE FIRST AND SECOND DAY OF THE month of *Tishri*. This celebration, which starts off a ten-day period leading to *Yom Kippur*, is known as the Ten Days of Penitence.

It is an important event, both spiritually and intellectually, because it provides an opportunity to assess one's actions and thoughts over the past year, and to question one's existence, choices and options in life. The liturgy, prayers and biblical texts read at this time all express man's inherent capacity to shake up his existence and find new, original paths.

Rosh Hashanah encourages people to pull themselves out of the daily routine, out of daily habits, and to let go of the weight of being. The continuation of this thinking is found ten days later in the celebration of *Yom Kippur*, which is like a confirmation of the decisions made during *Rosh Hashanah*.

The officiant is dressed in white to bring attention to the solemnity of the celebration, but it is by no means a sad event.

To foster inner searching, the *shofar* is blown several times each morning during prayer at the synagogue, as the sound of this horn stirs the being and puts it into question. Every man, woman and child listens to the blowing of the *shofar*. For people who are ill or unable to come to the synagogue (women who are having difficult pregnancies, for example), the community sends someone to sound the *shofar* at their homes.

The two evenings of *Rosh Hashanah* provide an occasion for unusual celebrations around the dinner table and particularly so in Sephardic households. Specially prepared dishes are used in expressing good wishes for the New Year. Ashkenazim communities, Jews originating from Eastern Europe, customarily dip slices of fresh apple into honey during these two evenings of celebration, saying "May this year be as sweet for us as this apple dipped in honey."

After the bread is blessed, it also is dipped in honey, not in salt, as is customary.

In Sephardic communities, made up of Jews from Spain and Portugal and their descendants, a true *seder* is organised: the table is sumptuously decorated and laid out with sweet dishes. Certain variations are found, depending on the country of origin, but the idea is essentially the same: to eat food over the next two nights whose Hebrew or

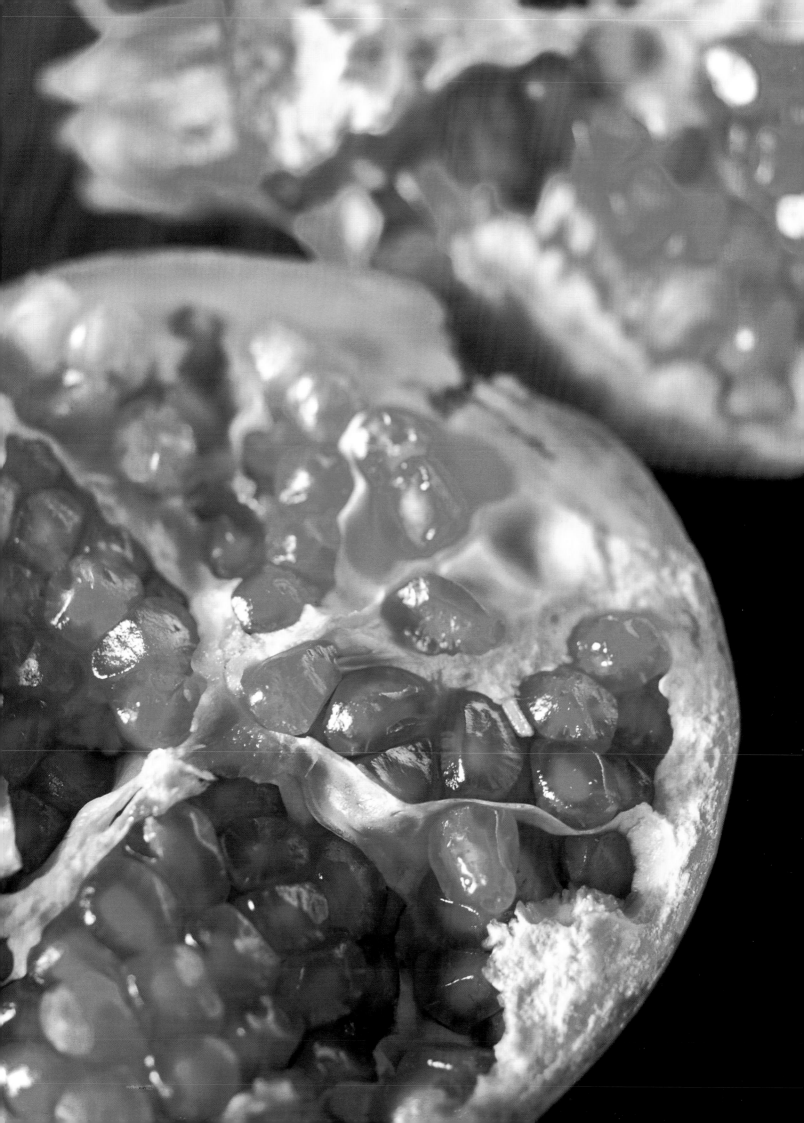

Aramaic names evoke biblical passages, either for blessing the Jewish people or for cursing its enemies. It is a play between food and words. The idea during *Rosh Hashanah* is "let's eat the book!" — an evening of "food for thought, thought for food".

Thus, on a Morrocan table, for example, you would be able to find:

– a fruit dish filled with fresh apples, and preferably red ones.

– a small jar of honey in which slices of apple are dipped: may the New Year be as sweet as the apple dipped in honey.

– a small bowl of sesame seeds mixed with granulated sugar: may we be as numerous as the grains of sesame.

– a dish of fresh dates: may all enemies vanish.

– a bowl of pomegranates sprinkled with orange-flower water: may our merits be as numerous as the pomegranate seeds.

– a dish filled with beets: may our enemies move far away from us.

– a dish with a lamb's head: may we always be ahead and not behind.

– a dish with one fish: like the fish, may we always have our eyes open, be on the look-out, and flourish in great number.

– a platter holding seven vegetables: carrots (may all poor decisions made about us be dropped), two types of squash (may all poor judgments be abandoned), chick peas, beets, onions and raisins.

– a bowl of green olives, for they are one of Israel's favourite fruits.

– the *Kiddush* glass.

– festive breads, also frequently dipped in honey.

– leeks, green beans, quince fruit, jujubes or grapes, may also be on the table, depending on the custom, as these seasonal fruits and vegetables are new, like the new year.

Happy new year, *Shanah Tova!*

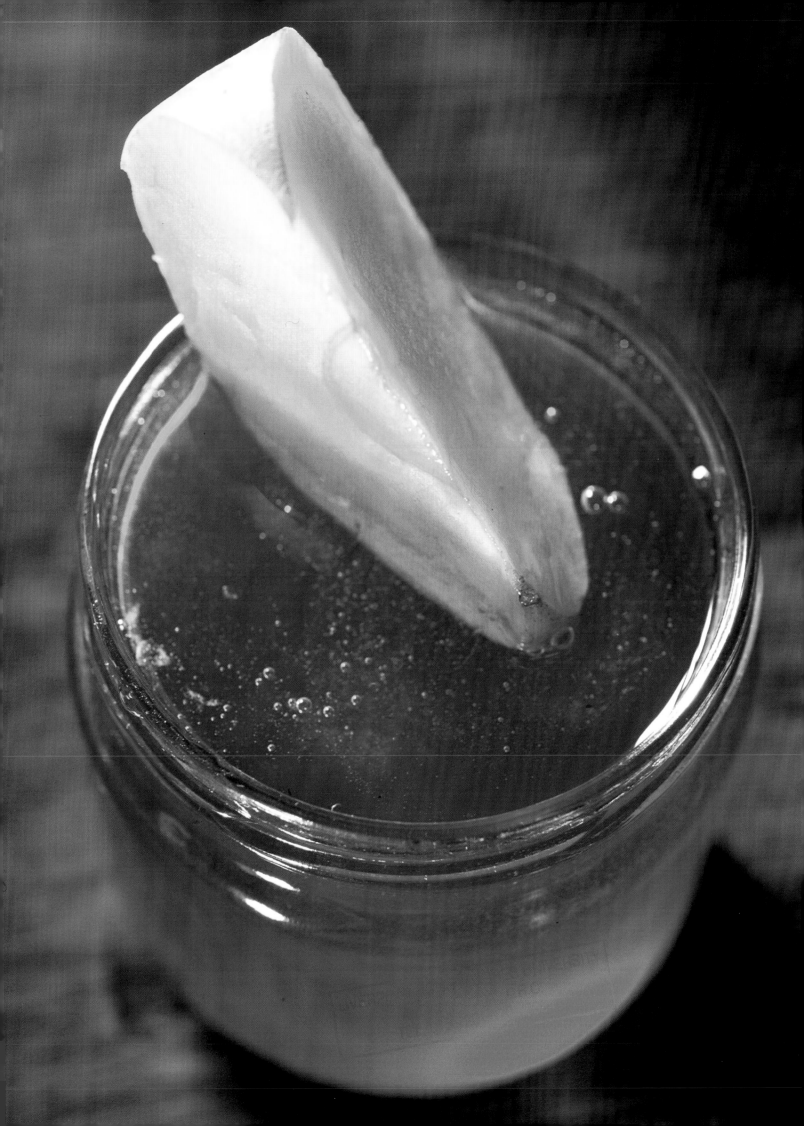

CHAPTER 11

YOM KIPPUR

THE DAY OF ATONEMENT

YOM *KIPPUR* OR IN ITS SHORT FORM, *KIPPUR*, IS THE DAY OF ATONEMENT. FOR JEWS AROUND THE WORLD, IT IS THE MOST WELL-KNOWN and revered holiday, as it is exceptional both psychologically and spiritually.

On this day, the human being is released from his past. No matter what mistakes, errors or violent acts he may have committed, he may now be pardoned. The man who decides to change, to question himself, to live in harmony with himself becomes free. He is forgiven, and he may now open himself up to the infinite nature of time. There are three essential paths to follow to arrive at this state of atonement;

1) prayer, in which mistakes are listed and atonement is sought;

2) fasting, in order to devote oneself entirely to this spiritual awakening;

3) charity, or *tzedaka*.

Yom Kippur is the apogee of Ten Days of Penitence which begins during *Rosh Hashanah*. It is a day of strict fasting, and lasts from sunset until nightfall the next day. It falls on the Hebraic date of *Tishri* 10, in September.

The day before the fast, it is customary to give money or food to the poor. To this end, collection boxes called *tzedaka* boxes are found all over the world, in Jewish stores, on the streets of Israel, dug into stone walls of houses or affixed to tree trunks. The day before *Kippur*, a ceremony called *kapparah* takes place in which a chicken or hen is swung three times over the head. Afterwards, the animal is slaughtered and given to the poor, or else the monetary value of the animal is donated. This is a symbolic way of ridding oneself of the weight of one's errors and mistakes. The same ceremony may also be performed using only money, without the animal.

Near mid-afternoon on the day before *Kippur*, a final meal is served before the fast. The woman of the household lights two candles, as she does for the Sabbath.

Five activities are banned during the *Kippur* fast: eating, drinking, washing, anointing oneself with oils, sexual relations, and wearing shoes with leather soles. Generally, shoes with plastic soles are worn, as no comfort should be sought on this day.

Everyone who has reached religious maturity is expected to take part in the fast. Five prayers are recited during the twenty-four hour fast. *Yom Kippur* ends with the sounding of the *shofar*, heard as an echo of both hope and freedom.

Collection boxes, or Tsedaka *boxes, to give money as an offering on the eve of Kippur, is one of the three fundamental actions, with prayer and fasting: "The* Tsedaka *saves from death" (Proverb 10,2)*

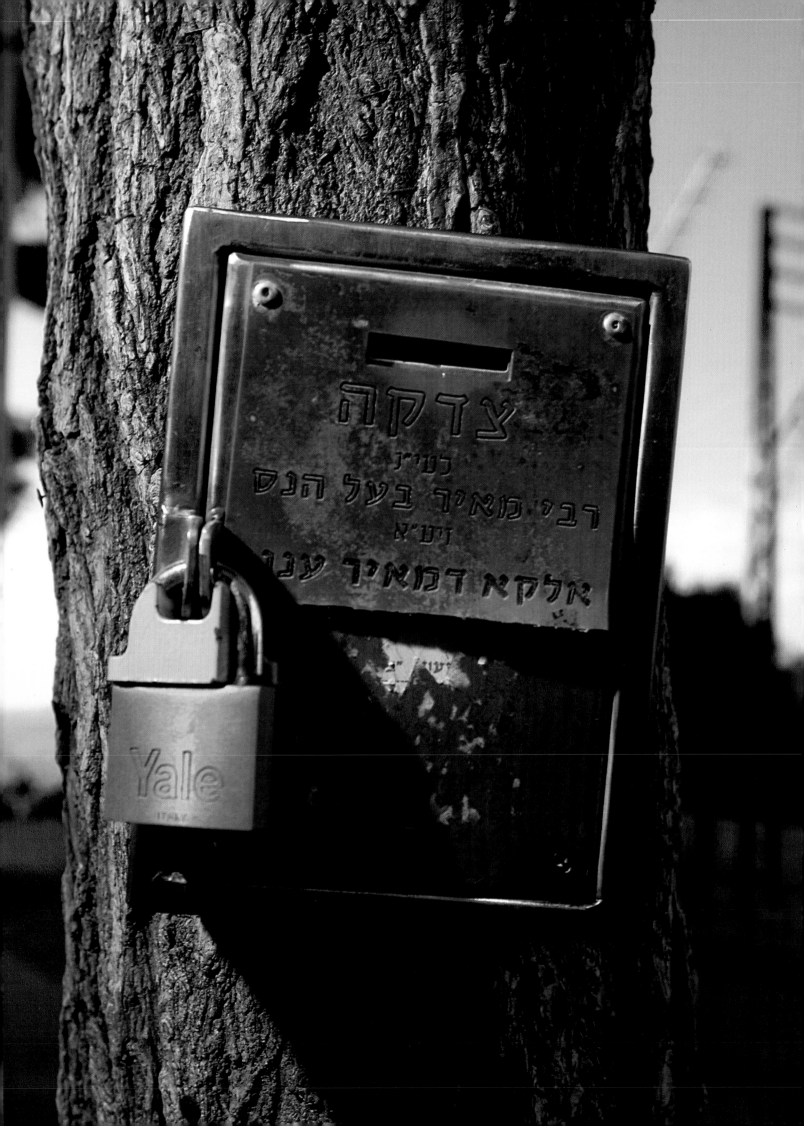

CHAPTER 12

THE SUCCAH

THE FESTIVAL OF BOOTHS

DURING THE CELEBRATION OF *SUCCOTH* OR THE FESTIVAL OF BOOTHS, THE THIRD PILGRIMAGE EVENT IN THE JEWISH YEAR, small booths called *succoth* (*succah* in the singular) are built outdoors. They are lived in for seven days, in memory of the forty years the Jews spent in the desert after the Exodus from Egypt.

The *succoth* Festival of Booths takes place after the celebration of *Rosh Hashanah* (the Jewish New Year) and *Kippur* (the Day of Atonement) during which the *shofar* rite is performed (see chapter nine). It lasts seven days in Israel, and eight in the Diaspora.

This celebration has in fact several different names: the Festival of Booths; the Feast of Tabernacles; the Harvest Festival; or the Time of Joy.

A booth is built that will stay up for the entirety of the holiday. The word *succah* is derived from *skhakh*, which is the thatching used for the roof. The booth is intended to look temporary, to represent the dwellings the Jews lived in as they wandered through the wilderness. It pays respect to living, and living precariously.

The aim behind the construction of the *succah* is to experience what it feels like to live in a dwelling which is in the process of being built, as opposed to a place which is already built. Each year, a new shelter must be constructed for the event (in Hebrew: *Taasse, velomine heassouye*).

The walls of the *succah* can be made of a solid immovable material. The roof should be built of cut vegetable material, such as wood, boards, rattan, reeds, pine, etc. There must be more shade than sunlight inside the *succah*.

The roof is the most important element of the *succah*. It is the *skhakh*, and gives its name to the entire living space inside. The roof does not represent a limit, but rather an invitation to go beyond. One must go beyond oneself.

It is no mere coincidence that the entire month of *Tishri*, the month in which *Succoth* takes place, is under the sign of the letter *lamed*, which symbolises moving beyond, as explained in chapter seven.

The way a human being thinks is very much a reflection of the way he lives.

In other words, one's manner of living on earth, just like that of living in space or the body, reveals as much about the spirit of man as it does one's ideas or behaviour.

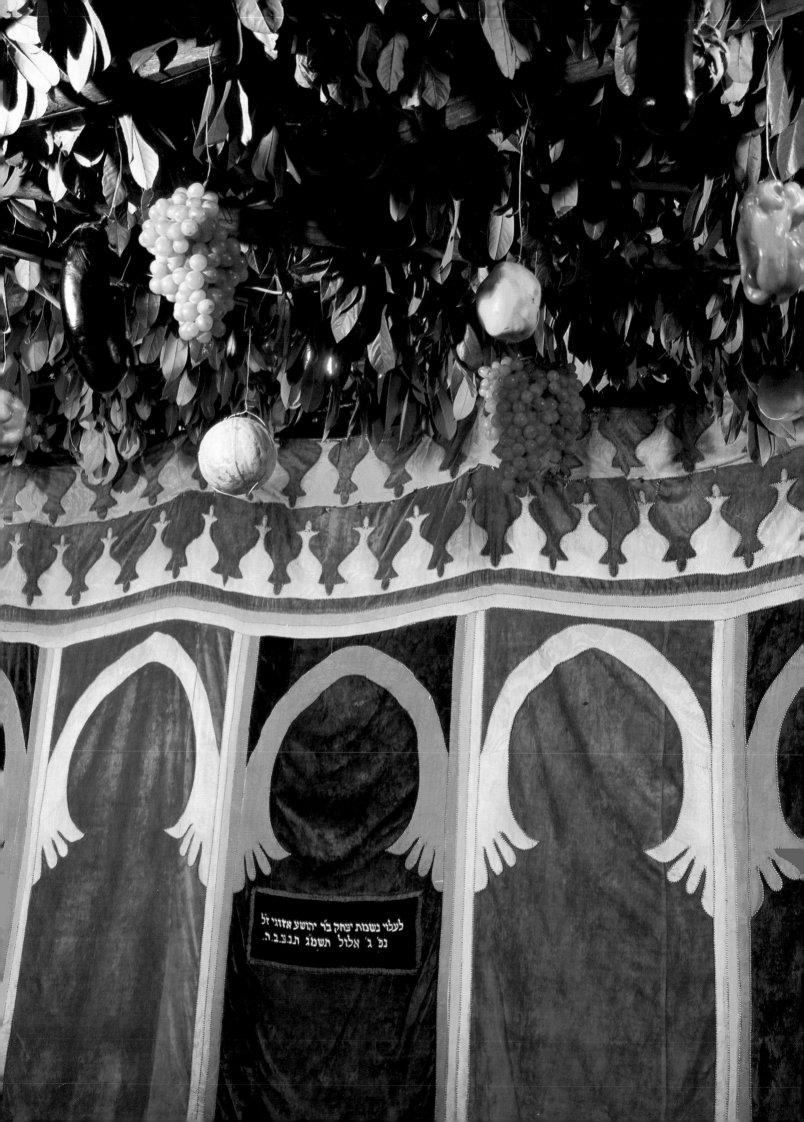

לעלוי נשמת יצחק ב"ר יהושע אזוגי ז"ל
נפ' ג' אלול תשמ"ג תנצב"ה.

CHAPTER 13

THE LULAV

THE LANGUAGE OF FLOWERS

THE OTHER RITE OF *SUCCOTH* IS THE *LULAV*. EACH DAY DURING THE CELEBRATIONS, A BOUQUET COMPOSED OF THE following elements is brought along to the morning prayer:

– the *etrog*: a fragrant citron

– the *lulav*: a palm branch

– the *hadassah*: three myrtle branches

– the *aravah*: two willow branches

The bouquet is named after of one of these elements: the *lulav.*

To give the blessing to this rite during the morning prayer, the *lulav* is held in the right hand, with the three myrtle branches positioned to the right of the palm branch, and the two willow branches to the left. These three branches are fastened together. The fragrant citron is held in the left hand. After the blessing of the rite, the two hands are brought together and the four plants are shaken up and down in the direction of the four cardinal points. The rite of the *lulav* is not performed on the day of the Sabbath. The origins of the *lulav* are associated with *Succoth*, which began as a celebration of agriculture called the Harvest Festival. It consists of thanking God for all species of vegetation.

The *lulav*, the palm tree, is a tree which bears fruit, but which has no natural perfume. The *hadassah*, the myrtle, does not bear any fruit, but has a natural heady perfume. The willow, the *aravah*, does not produce either fruit or a natural perfume, while the citron, the *etrog*, has both fruit and perfume. Meaning has been given to these symbols as a way of classifying the practitioner of the Jewish faith. A person may be defined by his knowledge of the *Torah* (perfume), by his practice of it (fruit), by reflection (perfume) and by action (fruit). The *lulav* bouquet represents the Jewish people in its diversity:

– people who practice and study the religion are represented by the fruit and perfume of the *etrog;*

– those who practice the religion without study are symbolised by the *lulav*, the palm branch;

– those who study and have the spirit of the *Torah* within them are represented by the myrtle branch;

– and finally, those who neither practice nor study are symbolised by the willow.

The bouquet functions as a whole in the rite, emphasising that everyone has as much value as the other if he or she works together with the others to build the community. The rabbi has as much importance as a simple follower; and a scholar should not be glorified for his knowledge. It is the joy of working together on a common project which is important. The *lulav* is a symbol of the unity and solidarity of the Jewish people.

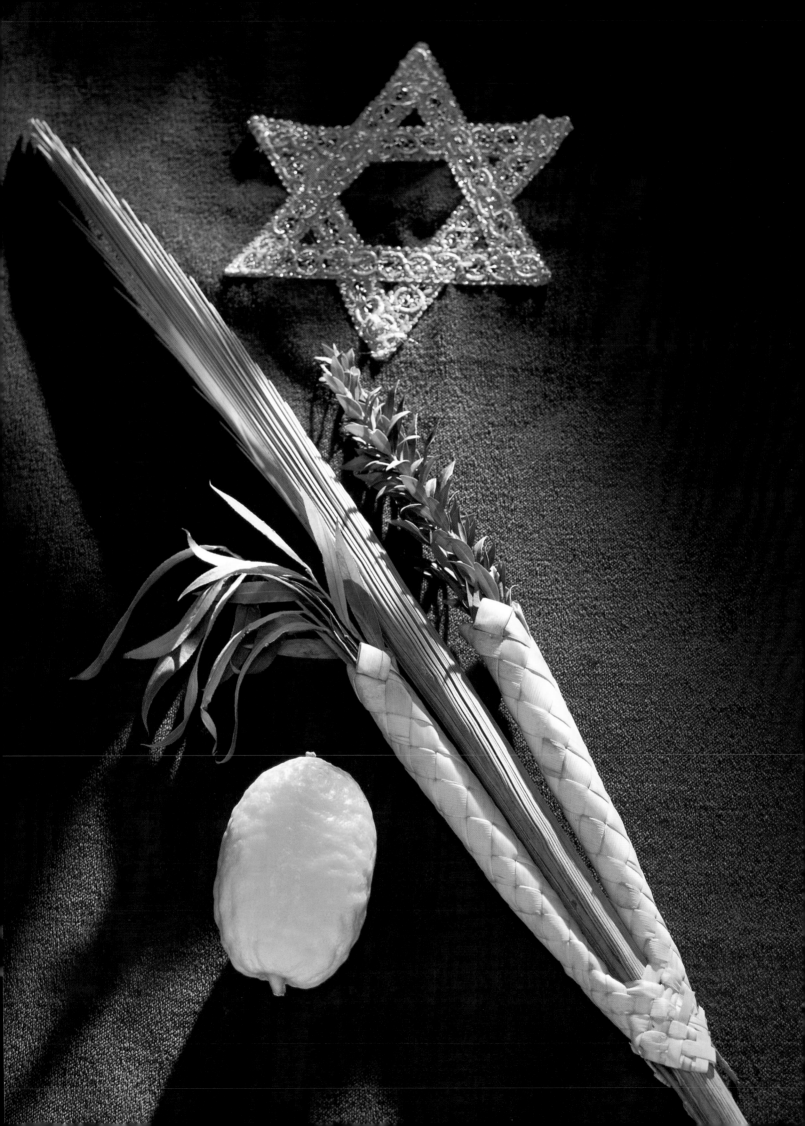

CHAPTER 14

HANUKKAH

A TREE OF LIGHT

IN THE SECOND CENTURY BEFORE THE CHRISTIAN ERA, THE JEWISH PEOPLE WON A LARGE MILITARY AND SPIRITUAL VICTORY over Greek universalism. The victory was cemented with the reclaiming of the Temple of Jerusalem. All sacrileges perpetrated by the occupiers were purged, and the candelabrum was lit once again — the symbol of restored light.

During the construction of the portable sanctuary in the desert, God ordered that certain religious objects be made, namely the *menorah*, a candelabrum with seven branches. The description given in the Bible (*Exodus* 25: 31-40) is like that of a tree of light. This candelabrum remained lit; it was an eternal light.

In Jewish history, this candelabrum took on a particularly important significance after an event occurred that is fundamental to the Jewish consciousness.

Judea had been under Persian domination until 333 B.C., when it fell to the Greeks who were led by Alexander the Great. After the death of Alexander the Great, his empire was divided up amongst his generals, one ruling in Egypt and the other in Syria. Following a war of spoils, Judea was controlled by the kingdom of Syria, ruled by the Seleucid dynasty.

Antiochus IV Epiphane, known as Epimane (the madman) by the Jews, rose to the throne of Syria in 175 B.C. (3585, according to the Jewish calendar). A hot-tempered tyrant who despised the Jewish religion, he wanted to unify his kingdom through the imposition of one religion and culture — Hellenism. The Jewish religion was banned, and scrolls of the *Torah* were confiscated and burned. Practicing the Sabbath, circumcision, and *kashrut* were punishable by death.

The Jews were divided amongst themselves. On the one hand stood the devout believers, or *Hassidim* who, refusing to follow the rules laid down by Antiochus, continued to study the *Torah* and observe the *Mitsvot*, despite threats of execution. On the other, the Hellenistic Jews were not opposed to assimilation with the Greek culture and religion. They abandoned the *Torah* and their religious practices and devoted themselves to art and the Olympic games, which at the time were religious in nature. And finally, there were the indecisive Jews, those who did not know whether they should join the *Hassidim* or the Hellenists.

In the small village of Modin, not far from Jerusalem, lived the old priest Mattathias, the father of five sons.

One day, Antiochus's soldiers arrived in

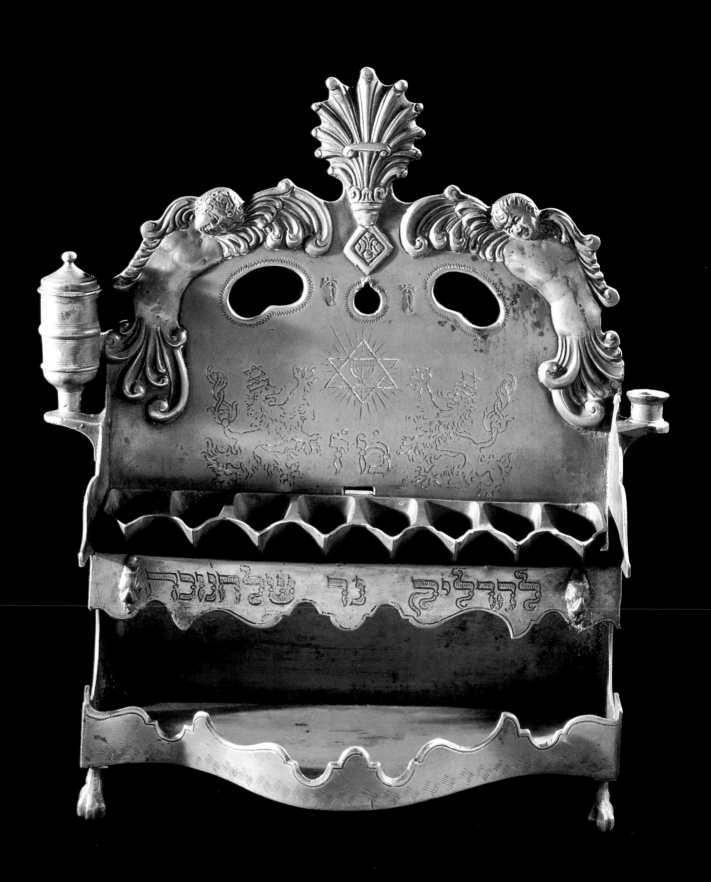

Mondin and erected an altar in the market square. They called the Jews to come forth and offer sacrifices to the Greek gods. The High Priest Mattathias spoke and said: "My sons, my brothers and I will remain faithful to the covenant of our fathers." At this moment, a Hellenistic Jew came forth to the altar to offer a sacrifice. Mattathias took his sword and killed him instantly, thus triggering a rebellion. The sons and the friends of Mattathias leapt on the Greek officers and soldiers, killing many of them, while others fled. The Jews demolished the sacrificial altar, and sought refuge in the mountains.

Soon the faithful Jews and the undecided Jews joined Mattathias and his sons in the mountains, and the rebellion became one of the entire Jewish people of Judea.

Before dying, the High Priest brought his five sons together, Johannes, Simon, Jonathan, Judah and Eleazar, and urged them to continue the combat. He appointed his son Judah head of the army, known as Judah Maccabee — *Makabi* signifies hammer, in other words, Judah the Hammer — for his bravery, or perhaps also because of the slogan printed on his standard: *Makabi* are the initials for: "Who is like You amongst the Powerful, O Eternel". The soldiers of Antiochus, who were led by Apolonius, Nicanor and Gorgias, all generals at the head of a strong army, were struck down and defeated one by one.

Finally, Judah and his men went to Jerusalem, which they liberated in 165 B.C. (3595 in the Jewish calendar). The Temple of Jerusalem had been made impure by the presence of idols. Judah

Maccabee's companions purged the Temple of all idols and impurities, built a new altar, and consecrated it on *Kislev* 25 of the year 3595.

This was the Dedication of the Temple, hence the name *Hanukkah*, meaning "dedication" in Hebrew. *Hanukkah* also means "they rest (from their enemies) on the 25th."

Having purified the Temple, or *Hamikdash*, the Maccabees wanted to light the perpetual light with seven branches. But it had been stolen by the Syrian Greeks. A temporary candelabrum was thus fashioned. But only one flask of pure oil was found to fuel it, one that carried the stamp of the High Priest. However, it kept the candles lit for eight days, rather than just one, as was usually the case. This miracle of the oil flask is at the origin of the lighting of the candles during *Hanukkah*. But the real miracle was the victory of a handful of Jews over strong and organised armies which had invaded the East. The candelabrum — the symbol of this spiritual and political victory — has left a profound mark on the consciousness of the Jewish people. Along with the Star of David, it has become the symbol par excellence of Judaism and the people of Israel.

This candelabrum, laden with history, is also the official emblem of the State of Israel, in addition to representing resistance and rebirth. In remembrance of the miracle of *Hanukkah*, Jews light a candelabrum during a period of eight days.

This rite has evolved since the initial lighting of the candles. It would have been logical to light a candelabrum with seven branches over a period of eight days. However, the rule prohibiting representation includes objects found in the Temple. The eight-day miracle inspired the design of a new candelabrum — this one with eight branches instead of seven.

A second change was made official: the lights (oil lamps or candles) are lit one by one, not all eight at the same time. Thus, one candle is lit the first day, a second the next, and so forth, until the eighth candle is lit on the eighth day.

This carries with it the idea of improvement, of continuous renewal. According to the principle set out by the school of Hillel: "One rises with holiness, and one does not descend."

The candle used to light the *Hanukkah* lights (thus making nine in the candelabrum) is called the *shammash*, "the servant"; it is placed on the side or in the centre, a little bit higher or slightly displaced from the candelabrum, so as not to be confused with the eight ritualistic candles.

According to the *Kabbalah*, the number of candles lit corresponds to the Name of God, EHYE, which is written out as *aleph-hay-yod-hay* and which means "I will be". It is a setting into motion of this name which means the future. The same relationship to language is found here, as in the "language in motion" concept discussed in the chapters concerning the *tallith* and the *mezuzah*.

The rites are, as such, the memory of historic events of the Jewish people and also the writing of the living name upon the physical matter of the world. The name EHYE written as *aleph-hay-yod-hay* equals the numbers 1-5-10-5.

If these figures are added according to the principal of lighting the *Hanukkah* candles, one arrives at the sum:

$$1$$
$$1+5$$
$$1+5+10$$
$$1+5+10+5$$
$$= 44$$

The same principle is applied to the candles. Every day during *Hanukkah*, forty-four candles (thirty-six candles and eight *shammash*) are lit, the numerical equivalent of the name "I will be".

The rite is a reminder in light that "the perfection of man lies in his perfectibility". It is interesting to note that all historical sources concerning *Hanukkah* are in Greek. Thus, the Jewish memory is transmitted by a language other than Hebrew, through another culture. This is perhaps another one of the lessons of *Hanukkah*: Light is only possible through dialogue between cultures, not through rejection, as an unsophisticated reading of history could lead one to believe. The lights of *Hanukkah* are like hands of light extended outwards in the name of dialogue and peace.

CHAPTER 15

TU BI-SHEBAT

THE NEW YEAR OF TREES
OR JEWISH ARBOUR DAY

TU BI-SHEBAT IS THE NEW YEAR OF TREES, CELEBRATED BY A FEAST OF FRUIT AND BY THE PLANTING OF NEW TREES. IN HEBREW, *Tu* equals the number 15. The entire word *Tu Bi-Shebat* means the fifteenth of the month of *Shebat*, which generally falls around February.

The New Year of Trees is one of four New Year's celebrations during the Jewish year. It is a happy event, helping mark the end of winter. During festivities, at least fifteen types of fruit are laid out on the table. The seven most important are those which grow in Israel (*Shibah ha-Minim*): wheat, barley, grapes, pomegranates, figs, dates and olives. A place of honour is also given to fruit from the carob tree, which was abundant in Israel when the festival was inaugurated, and to almonds. The almond tree is the first tree to grow buds at the end of winter, and is in full bloom in the middle of *Shebat*.

Some communities, following a mystical tradition, sing hymns especially written for each of the seven types of fruit.

In the same tradition, four goblets of wine composed of mixtures of red and white wine are drunk in the following order: the first goblet is filled with red wine, the second contains two-thirds red wine and one third white, the third holds one-third red wine and two-thirds white, and the fourth is filled with white wine.

Red represents rigour, *din*, and white stands for generosity, *hessed*. The four goblets of wine represent a range of possible combinations of behaviour which run from the strictest rigour, to the most open generosity.

But the ideal is a balance between *din* and *hessed*, between rigour and generosity, a balance which can only be found after all other possibilities have been exhausted.

To embellish the occasion, the rarest and most exotic fruits are sought out — the more kinds of fruit on the table, the better.

In Israel, *Tu Bi-Shebat* is a time when schoolchildren plant thousands of young trees in forests. Their efforts have helped turn the desert green! *Tu Bi-Shebat* is an ecological celebration — bringing man closer to nature, teaching him to respect and care for it. Jews compare the human being to a tree which grows and bears fruit. During wars, for example, cutting trees to make a fence or a weapon is forbidden.

Make trees, not war!

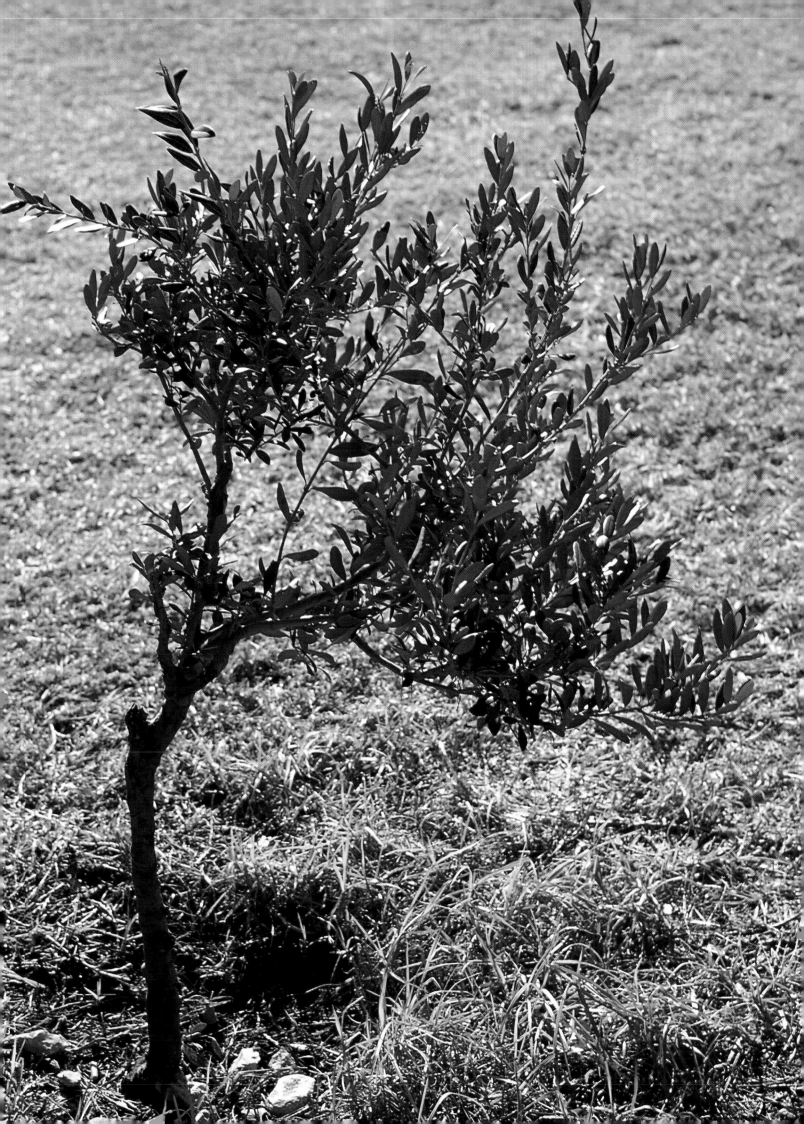

CHAPTER 16

THE MEGILLAH

THE SCROLLS OF ESTHER.
PURIM: COSTUME AND CARNIVAL

PURIM, OR THE FEAST OF LOTS, IS THE JEWISH CARNIVAL, CELEBRATING THE VICTORY OF THE JEWS OF PERSIA OVER HAMAN, THE anti-Semite. The Scroll of Esther, or *Megillah*, is read during *Purim*, and a party is held which everyone attends dressed up in costume.

Purim takes place on *Adar* 14, according to the Jewish calendar (around March) and celebrations revolve around the reading of the story of Esther in the *Megillah Esther*, which is found in the third part of the Bible. The *Megillah* is a text written entirely by hand with a reed or a goose quill on a roll of parchment paper kept in a box. Both the *Megillah* and the box have been an inspiration to many artists re-creating objects of the Jewish faith.

The Scroll of Esther is read twice during *Purim* celebrations, once the evening before *Adar* 14, and a second time the next morning — when children attend and people come dressed in cos-tume. *Purim* is at the origin of Mardi Gras. It is a celebration of freedom and joy marking the rescue of the Jews from being massacred by Haman. At that time, Jews who lived in exile, following the destruction of the Temple in 586 of the pre-common era, went even as far as Persia, where they lived peacefully among the native people. One day, Haman appeared, a recently-named vizier who detested Jews and swore he would see to it that every one of them was exterminated.

Haman chose the date for the massacre of the Jews of Persia by drawing or casting "lots", hence the name *Purim*, or Feast of Lots. The date indicated was the 14th of the month of *Adar*.

Haman, who was first Minister of King Ahasuerus (possibly Artaxerxes II), received the King's approval. But the King's wife, Esther, who was Jewish, aided by the sagacity of her uncle Mordecai, delivered the Jews. Esther, Mordecai and all the Jewish people had fasted for three days

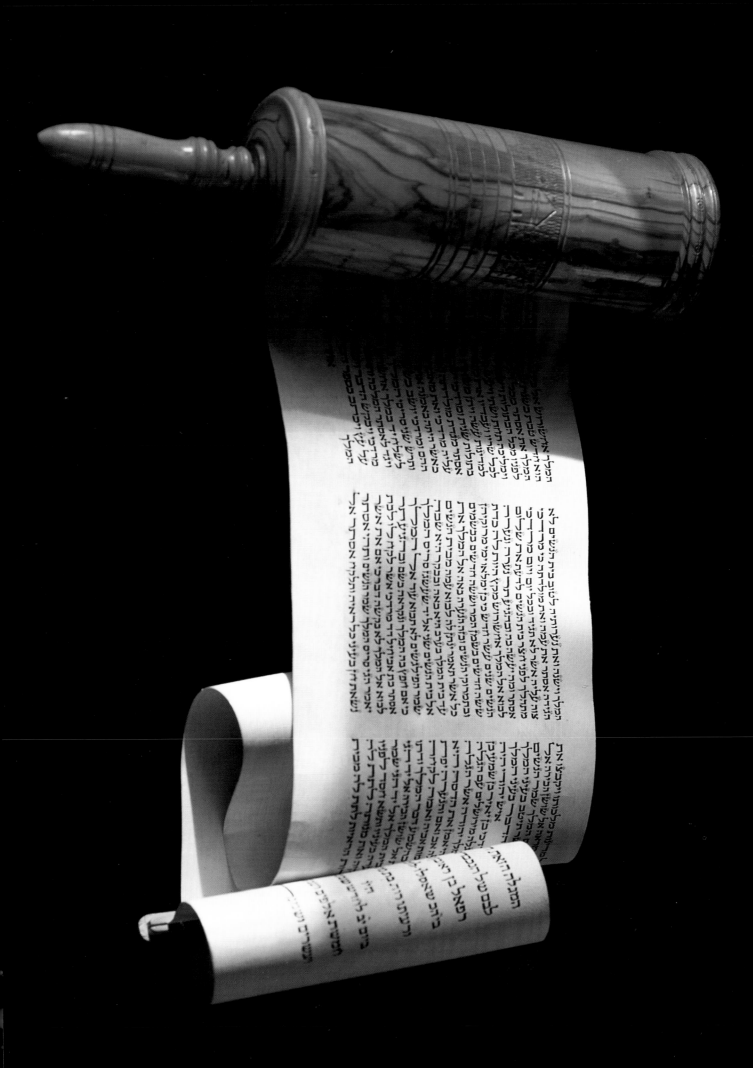

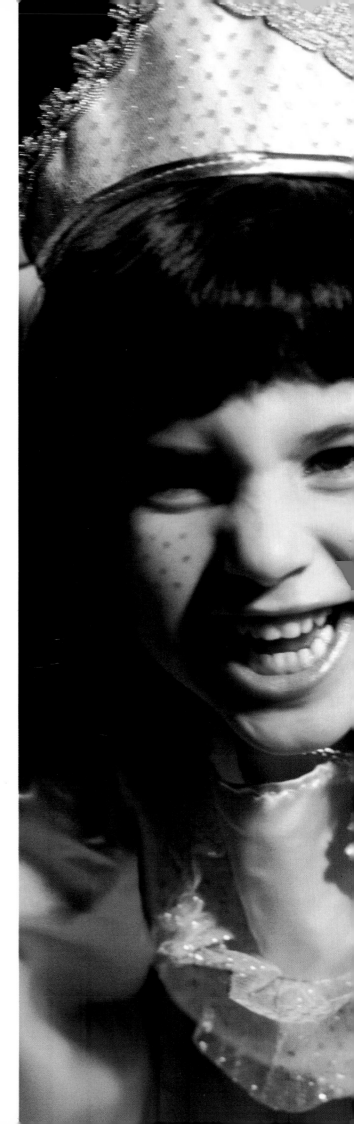

in a row. Thanks to their combined efforts in influencing the King, the Jews were saved and Haman and his son were hanged.

The fast of Esther is held on *Adar* 13 to commemorate that historic fast. And the miraculous liberation of the Jewish people is marked by *Purim*, a happy event celebrated by dressing up in costumes, enjoying feasts, exchanging gifts, and giving donations to the poor.

For *Purim*, *Hamantash* (Haman's ears), delicious baked pastries filled with nuts, raisins, poppy seeds, or other ingredients, are baked in communities in the West. Eating, drinking and revelling are encouraged during *Purim*, with everyone dressed up in costume, trying to be as anonymous as possible. During *Purim*, the Jews were transformed miraculously from being a persecuted people to a protected people, and from being despised to being honoured. The idea behind dressing up is to look entirely different from one's habitual appearance. Who is respected, who is despised? Who is Jewish, who is Haman? Mixing up identities allows each person to reinvent himself, and to be freed from the prison they may have been enclosed in.

The Masters of the *Talmud* say that the miracle of the *Purim* was a miracle where God was hidden, or remained very discrete. In the text of the *Megillah*, God's name does not appear at all. The story is presented as a tale of men who take destiny into their own hands. In fact, the name Esther means: "that which is hidden". It is this element of hiding that also exists in the practice of dressing up in costume.

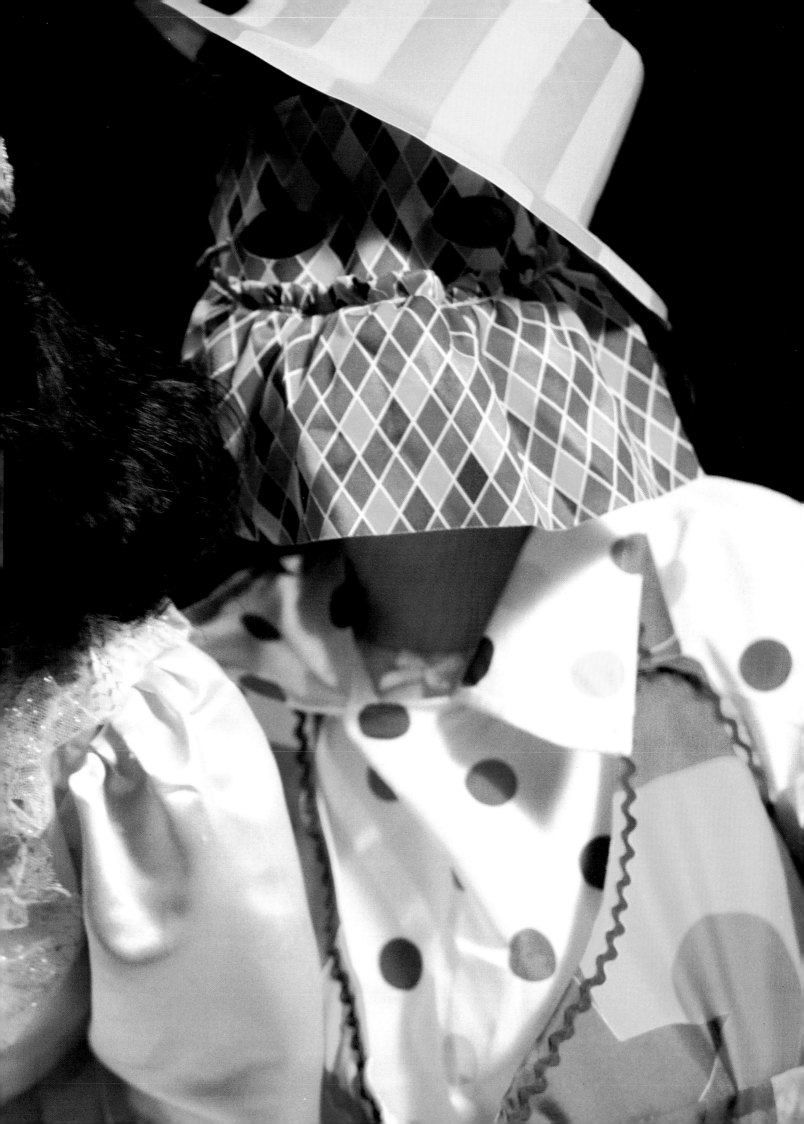

CHAPTER 17

PESACH

THE JEWISH EASTER.
"REMEMBER THE EXODUS FROM EGYPT"

PASSOVER FESTIVITIES LAST SEVEN OR EIGHT DAYS, AND DURING THIS TIME IT IS FORBIDDEN TO EAT ANYTHING CONTAINING YEAST. Unleavened bread or *matzah* is eaten instead of regular bread, and the festivities begin with a special meal called the *seder*. *Pesach* is one of the three pilgrimage celebrations, along with *Shebuoth* and *Succoth*. It falls on *Nisan* 15, which is generally in the month of April, and lasts eight days (seven in Israel). The first and last two days are holidays, and the days in between are partial holidays, called *hol ha-mœd*.

Pesach is a celebration that is both religious and agricultural in origin. It marks the arrival of spring and of the first barley harvest. It also commemorates the Exodus of the Hebrews from Egypt and the end of slavery. It is important to remember and mark this occasion, as it is one of the major events in Jewish history.

Jews had been slaves for over 400 years until Moses awakened in them a desire for freedom. The Pharoah kept them in bondage until ten epidemics were sent down as divine punishment, those of blood, frogs, lice, flies, the pestilence, boils, hail, locusts, darkness, and death of the first-born.

The word *Pesach* means "to pass over", as God passed over the homes of the Hebrews during the tenth plague of Egypt, sparing the lives of their newborn. *Pesach* could be pronounced "Peh-Sa'h" if read aloud, meaning "the mouth which speaks".

It is a mandatory part of *Pesach* celebrations to tell the story of the Exodus from Egypt, as well as other stories which relate to the Exodus.

There are several activities which are forbidden during *Pesach*, just as there are duties (*Mitzvot*) which must be performed. One cannot eat, have in the home, or even look at *hamez*, which is anything containing yeast, and also by extension of that rule, any food containing flour or any of the cereals wheat, barley, oatmeal, spelt and rye, as these are cereals which ferment.

Instead, bread without yeast or unleavened bread, *matzah*, is eaten. It is a symbol of freedom, as it was the bread prepared by the Hebrews the day before the Exodus from Egypt, bread which never rose. *Matzah* also represents misery, as it was often consumed by the Hebrews when they were in bondage in Egypt.

The third mandatory element of the celebration is the *seder* of *Pesach*. During the *seder*, the story of the Exodus from Egypt is read from the *Haggadah*, and food symbolising the main aspects of the story are laid out on a platter and served as the main dish of the meal.

Discussing freedom is a manner of celebrating the fact one has the freedom to discuss. It is a way of talking about oneself, and of reinventing oneself at the same time.

Several very important preparations are made before the *seder*. All *hamez* found in the

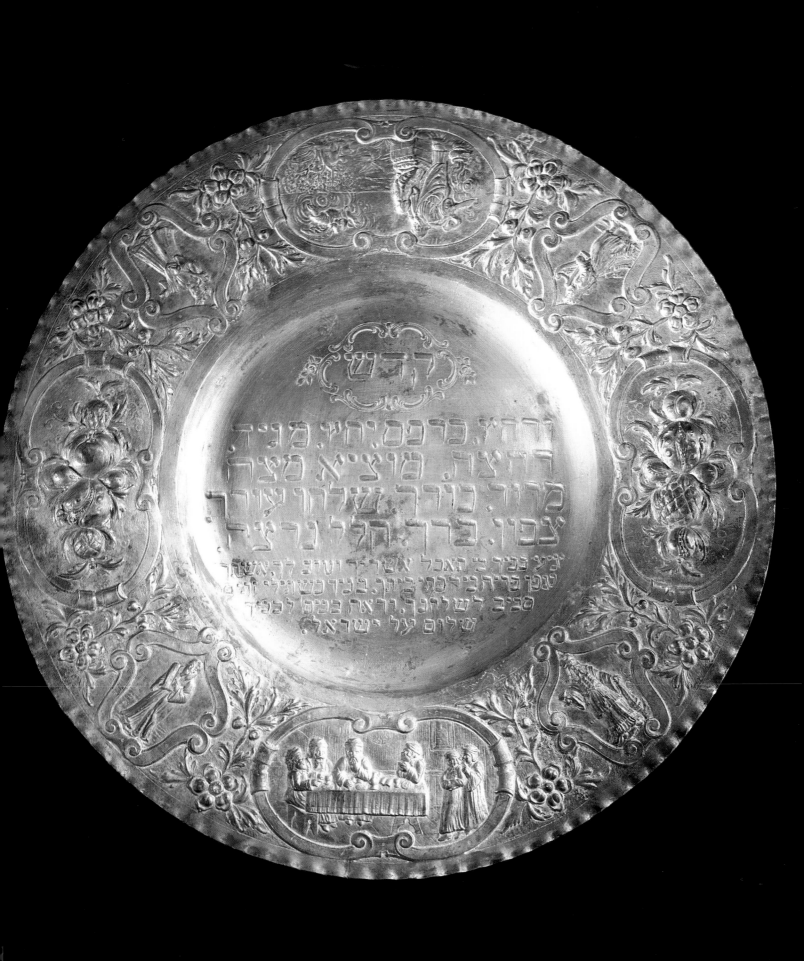

קדש

ברוך יהוה מנך.
דהוצת מוצא מצ׳
מרור נורל שלחו עורך
צפון ברך הלל נרצה.

מע נגד לי האכל אשרי ושרף לראשך
גפן פריתניכתי יהת בעדן שוגלי זה
סביב לשלהן. וראה בנח לבך
שלום על ישראל.

house, the car, the workplace, or anywhere else, is thrown out. A derivitive of these "cleanings" takes place today even among non-Jews, in the form of "spring cleanings".

The evening of *Nisan* 13, at nightfall, *Bedikat Hamez* takes place: a meticulous search for *hamez* throughout the entire house takes place by candlelight. Any *hamez* is burned the next morning during the *Bi'ur hamez* ceremony. *Hamez* is put on sale before *Bi'ur hamez* as a way of encouraging people to search thoroughly to be certain they haven't any left in the house by accident. On *Nisan* 14, the oldest boys in each household must fast in remembrance of the death of the first born in Egypt and of the saving of the Israelite first born. If the boy is not yet of age, his father must fast in his place.

The evening of *Nisan* 14, everyone gathers around the dinner table, where the main dish of the *seder* is the central focus.

THE *SEDER*: THE EVENING OF PASSOVER. THE MAIN DISH OF THE *SEDER*.

On a large dish, several symbolic elements are displayed, which are tasted and discussed throughout the Passover evening.

This is a very family-oriented evening. The word *seder* means "order", as everything takes place in a very specific order throughout the evening, which is detailed in a text read like a programme during the meal.

A copy of this text, called the *Haggadah* of *Pesach* is handed out to everyone at the table. It is one of the best-selling Jewish texts, and has inspired many Jewish artists. The main dish of the *seder* is placed in the middle of the table. All elements to be served throughout the course of the evening are laid out on the platter. The idea of the evening is to dramatise the elements associated with the Exodus from Egypt, in order to experience the event more profoundly, and to experience the feeling of what it was actually like to live during the liberation.

Questioning is a major part of the *seder*, especially concerning the existence of children. The questions focus on the unusual objects and customs which take place during Passover. For example, why is *matzah* eaten? Why are bitter herbs and vegetables used? Why must one eat and drink leaning to the left?

Several sentences of the *Haggadah* begin with the Hebrew word "*Mah*" to emphasise the importance of questioning, "*Mah*" meaning "what". For example, the word is found at the beginning of the well-known passage of the four questions. Children wait impatiently for this text to be read aloud, so they can all chant together "Why is this night different from the others?". This is one of the questions the *Haggadah* tries to answer throughout the evening.

The main dish of the *seder* contains the main symbols of Passover: a shankbone; a hard-boiled egg; a cup of salted water; a type of paste called *haroset*; bitter herbs and vegetables known as *maror* (usually horseradish is used, but Romaine lettuce, radishes or endives may also be served); herbs with leaves known as *karpas* (parsley or celery) and in the middle of the platter are three loaves of un-

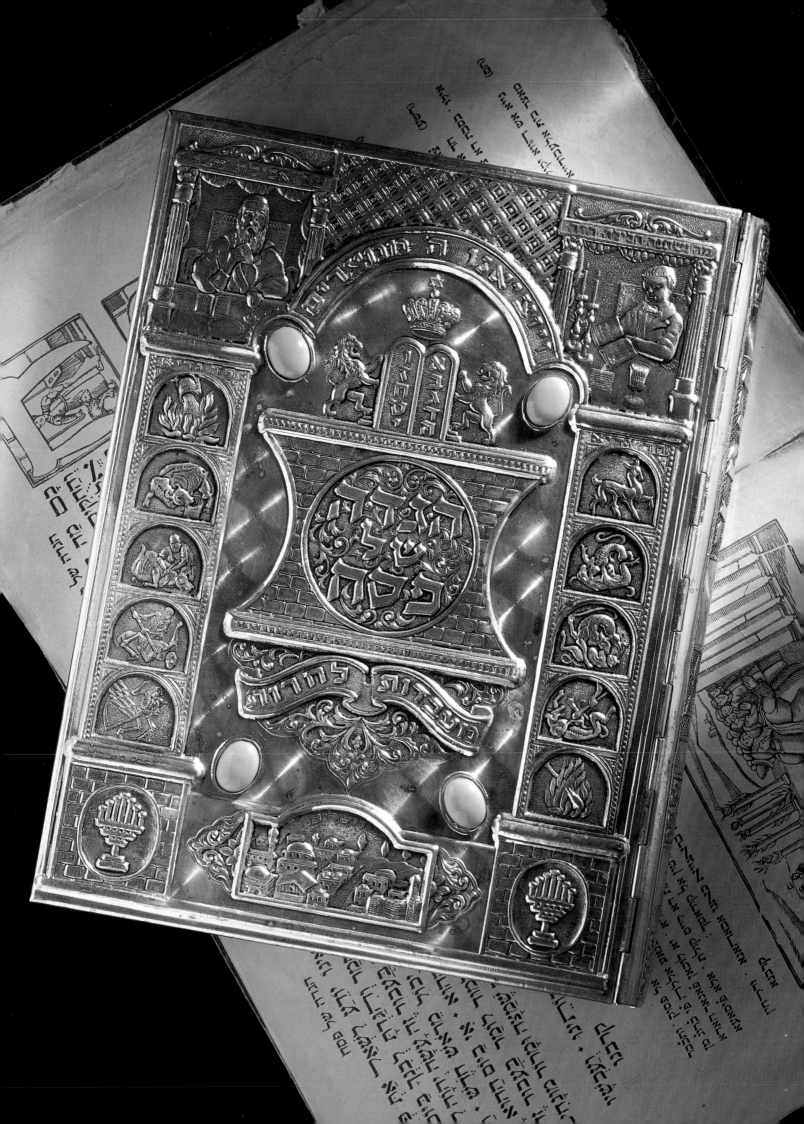

leavened bread. The location of each one of these items on the platter varies according to local custom.

THE MEANING OF THE SYMBOLS:

1. The shankbone signifies the sacrifice of the Passover lamb the evening before the Exodus from Egypt. Blood from the lamb was used to draw marks over the outside doors of Jewish houses so their newborn would be spared from death. (The description of this event is found in the book of *Exodus* in the Bible, chapters XII onward). The sacrifice of this lamb was the first sign of freedom for the Hebrews, for the lamb was a god to the Egyptians. To the enslaved people, the sacrifice of a god was an enormous gesture of trust and hope.

2. The hard-boiled egg signifies the sacrifice which was carried to each pilgrimage festivity. It is also a symbol of mourning for the destruction of the Temple of Jerusalem.

3. *Haroset* is a paste made from crushed apples mixed with nuts, cinnamon, red wine and ginger, or dates, nuts and apples. It represents the bricks the Hebrews made to build cities and monuments for the Pharoah.

4. *Maror*, bitter herbs and vegetables, whether Romaine lettuce, endives, radishes, black radishes, or horseradish, according to the community's custom. It is a reminder of the bitterness of slavery, as the Egyptians did more than just over-work the Hebrews. They degraded them psychologically and physically, beating them and forcing them to live under conditions that were so

precarious, it was as if the Hebrews themselves were delivering their children to a certain death.

5. *Karpas*, a herb with leaves, that is usually either parsley or celery, which represent the leaves used to smear the blood of the *Pesach* lamb over the doors of Hebrew homes.

6. The salt water in goblets represents the sweat and tears of the enslaved Hebrew people in Egypt.

7. The *matzoh*. There are three loaves, symbolising the three patriarchs, Abraham, Isaac, and Jacob, or else the three groups of Jewish people: the Cohen, Levi and Israel. During the *seder*, four glasses of wine are drunk, representing the four languages of freedom used in the Bible to recount the Exodus from Egypt. To further emphasise the importance of the liberation and freedom, the four glasses of wine are drunk leaning on the left elbow, because during the time the *seder* was instituted (the Roman era) only free men could recline on sofas as they ate.

The end of the *seder* is marked by the eating of the *afikoman*, a small piece of the *matsah* which was hidden and then found. The word *afikoman* originates from the Greek, and means dessert, but the Hassidic masters have traced the etymology of the word to the Armaic phrase "Bring on the questioning!" (*Afiqou-name*).

The *seder* ends with the singing of songs, the most well-known being the story of the "lamb my father bought for tuppence...". After the second evening of *Pesach*, each night is counted for a forty-nine day period. This continues until *Shebuoth* (Pentecost). This period is called the *omer*.

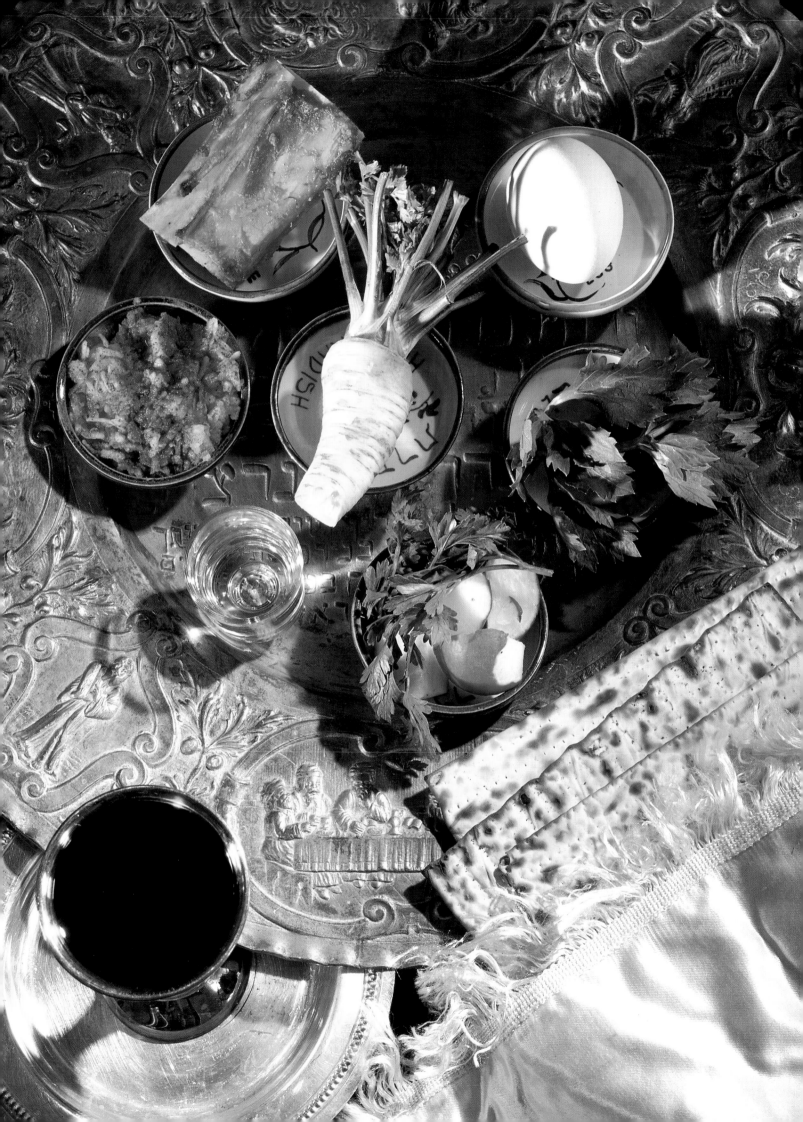

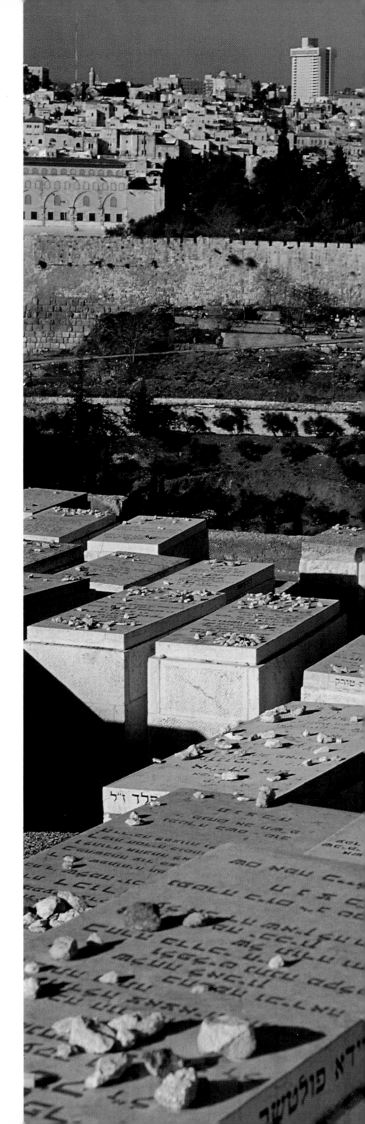

CHAPTER 18

LAG BAOMER

THE PILGRIMAGE TO
THE TOMB OF THE SAINTS.
THE SYMBOLS OF MOURNING
AND CONSOLATION.

THE PERIOD OF FORTY-NINE DAYS BETWEEN
PESACH (PASSOVER) AND *SHEBUOTH* (JEWISH
PENTECOST) IS CALLED THE *OMER*. THE
thirty-third day of this period is called the *Lag
BaOmer* and is commemorated by a series of
pilgrimages and rustic festivities. The word *omer*
has a number of meanings. During biblical times,
an *omer* designated a sheaf of new barley. The
forty-nine days — seven weeks — between *Pesach*
and *Shebuoth* is called *omer* because an *omer* of
barley was brought as an offering of the first fruits
of the harvest to the Temple starting on the
second day of the Passover holidays.

Lag *BaOmer* is the thiry-third day of the *omer*
period. *Lag* written in Hebrew is *lamedgimel*. *Lamed*
has a numerical value of thirty and *gimel* a
numerical value of three, therefore *lag* = 30 + 3 =
33 and *Lag BaOmer* is the thirty-third day of the
omer. The *omer* was originally a very joyous obser-

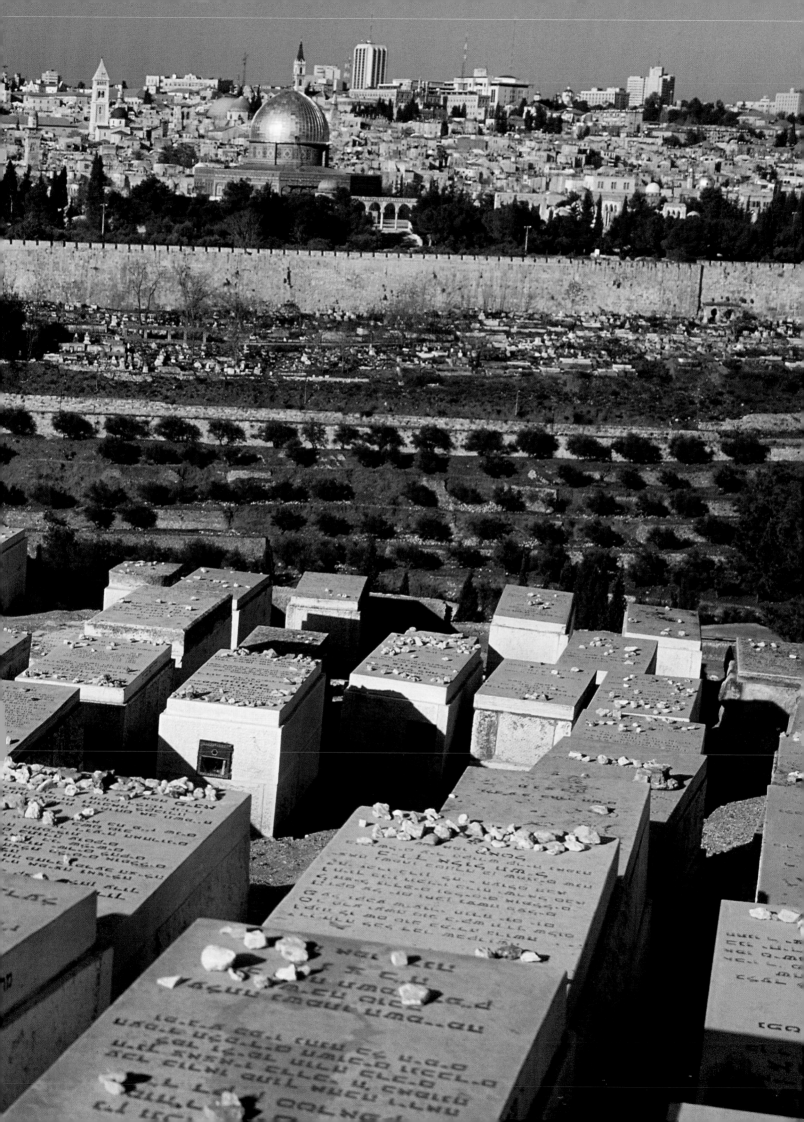

vance of the period of waiting leading up to the Feast of the Revelation of the *Torah*. This is the period between the Exodus from Egypt and the revelation of the *Torah* forty-nine days later, during which the Hebrews prepared themselves to receive the Law. And the days during which the Temple was being built constituted a period of joy and celebration linked to the harvest.

After the destruction of the Temple, the *omer* became a period of mourning and marriages were forbidden during its observance. How did this come about? According to various schools of thought, several different reasons can be given. We will only cite a few here.

In the year 132 of the common era, Israel was under Roman occupation. Certain Jews formed resistance movements and a revolt — a last attempt at independence — broke out under the leadership of Bar Kokhba. Rabbi Akiva, one of the most eminent masters of the *Talmud*, supported the revolt because he believed Bar Kokhba to be the Messiah. But the Romans crushed the insurrection and Bar Kokhba succumbed at Bethar in 135 after a heroic defence.

Following this, the Romans massacred ten great masters of the *Talmud*, including Rabbi Akiva. The failure of this revolt and the loss of these ten great talmudic figures are mourned during the *omer*.

We mourn for another reason, also in connection with Rabbi Akiva. Rabbi Akiva was the leader of thousands of disciples who brought glory to Israel. But they fell prey to a plague epidemic during the period of the *omer*, which miraculously ended on the thirty-third day. This is why *Lag BaOmer* is a half holiday.

This same day is considered to be the anniversary of the death of Rabbi Shimon bar Yohai, one of the great founders of the *Kabbalah*. It is therefore customary to make a pilgrimage to his tomb in Meron, a small locality next to Safed in Galilee. The pilgrimage is named the *hillula* of Rabbi Shimon bar Yohai and is still celebrated throughout the world through rustic excursions and pilgrimages to the tombs of the Saints.

It is customary to place a small stone on the tombs of saints or of any person one is visiting. This practice has several origins, one of which can be derived from a word play. The word "stone" in Hebrew is pronounced *eve* and written *aleph-bet-noun*. These three letters also represent "father": *av* and "son": *ben* which, when written together, form the word *even*, meaning stone. By placing a stone on the tomb we situate ourselves as a son of the deceased, as part of his bloodline and memory.

CHAPTER 19

THE KADDISH

THE PRAYER OF THE DEAD AND
SANCTIFICATION OF GOD'S NAME. THE SYMBOLS
OF MOURNING AND CONSOLATION.

THE *KADDISH*, ONE OF THE MOST WIDELY-KNOWN JEWISH PRAYERS, IS RECITED DURING MOURNING. ITS TRUE MEANING IS THE SANCtification of God's name, which continues to be honoured despite suffering and mourning. Different customs are followed at the passing away of a loved one: the covering of mirrors; taking off of one's shoes; even sitting on the floor.

The *Kaddish*, a very old prayer written in Aramaic, is a magnificent hymn to the greatness of God. Before being incorporated into the synagogal liturgy, it was originally recited at the closing of the study period. Its function is the separation and articulation of the different parts of prayer.

Later on, the *Kaddish* was also recited by those in mourning at the tomb of their parents or loved ones. It must then be recited during the eleven months which follow the death of an intimate, three times a day, at morning, afternoon and evening services and in the presence of ten people or the *minyan*. Even though the *Kaddish* does not, in itself, contain any reference to death, a passage evoking the resurrection of the dead is added at the burial ceremony. The *Kaddish* is, above all, a hymn of praise to God, signifying "holiness", from the word *kaddosh*, meaning "holy". Those in mourning speak of God's greatness, inviting God Himself to take care of the deceased and to welcome them into the other world untormented. The *Kaddish* has become a popular prayer, synonymous with consolation. It is customary for boys, notably the eldest son, to recite this prayer. In Yiddish, the eldest son is called *kaddish*, as he has the privilege of being called upon to recite this hymn of praise. When a person dies without leaving a child, it is said that he has not left a *kaddish*. Nowadays, it is customary for men as well as women to recite the *Kaddish*.

At the announcement of someone's death, whether the deceased is a loved one or not, one says the benediction *Barukh Dayan HaEmet*: "Praised are You, the True Judge". When a person dies, their loved ones must tear one of their articles of clothing. After the burial, those in mourning go either to the home of the deceased or to another house where it will be possible to respect a seven-day mourning period and have a meal of bread and hard-boiled eggs. Other members of the community provide this meal as a sign of their compassion and solicitude.

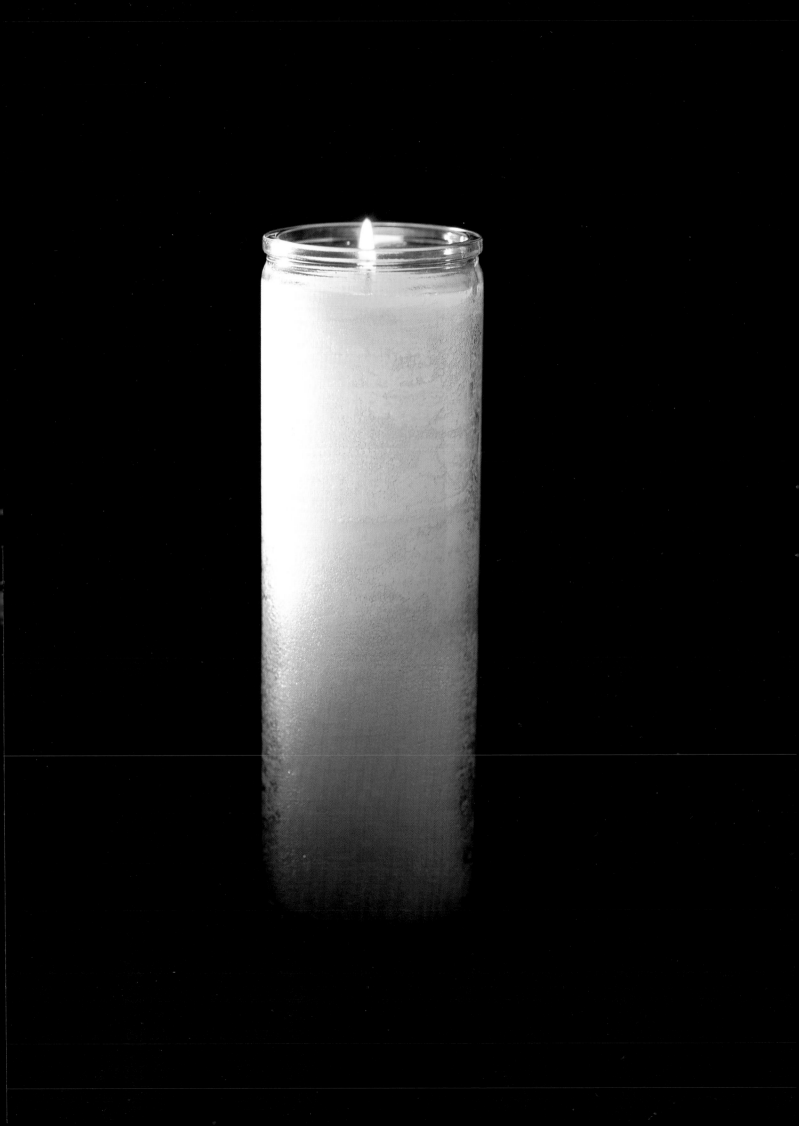

CHAPTER 20

SHEBUOTH

THE DONATION OF THE LAW AND
THE *YESHIVAH*: THE RABBINICAL ACADEMY

SHEBUOTH IS THE FESTIVAL OF THE REVE-
LATION OF THE *TORAH*, OTHERWISE KNOWN
AS THE TEN UTTERANCES OR TEN COMMAND-
ments. It is one of the three pilgrimage festivals.
The word *Shebuoth* signifies "weeks" as the festival
falls at the end of the period of *omer*, the seven
weeks of religious observance which starts with
the festival of *Pesach* (Passover).

According to the Hebrew calendar, this
festival falls on the sixth day of *Sivan*, generally in
the month of June, and lasts a day in Israel and
two days in the Diaspora. *Shebuoth* combines the
Festival of the Revelation of the *Torah* with the
celebration of First Fruits and the Grain Harvest
festival. It is a day on which all the synagogues
and houses are decorated with green foliage,
flowers, fruits and plants.

The Revelation of the *Torah* took place in
the desert on Mount Sinai. The Hebrews who
had gathered at the foot of the mountain received
the Ten Commandments which were engraved
on the Tablets of the Law carried by Moses.
Tradition tells us that on that day the Hebrews
received the entire *Torah* with all the commandments. There are 613 commandments in all,
consisting of 365 prohibitions and 248 mandatory
commandments. These constitute the fundamental principles of Judaism and regulate the life of
the Jew in the context of family, society and his
or her surroundings.

At the morning synagogue prayer during
Shebuoth, the Ten Commandments reading is
supplemented with a reading from the book of
Ruth, a pastoral evocation of the grain harvests.

It is customary during this festival to con-
sume chiefly lactic foods. There are several reasons
for this, one of which is linked to the white colour
of milk, a symbol of purity. Another possible
explanation links this tradition to the date of the
festival at the beginning of summer, when lighter
foods are eaten. And there is yet another: on the
sixth of *Sivan*, the Hebrews received the *Torah* as
well as all the recommendations concerning the
ritual slaughter of animals and the separation of
carnal and milk foods. At that time, there was
neither meat fit for consumption nor the proper
utensils to prepare it. The Hebrews, therefore, ate
lactic foods, which did not need long preparation.

It is also said that the sixth of *Sivan* is the
date on which the baby Moses was saved from the
Nile River by the Pharoah's daughter, and that he
would only be nursed with milk from a Jewish
woman. Traditionally, the entire night of *Shebuoth*
until the small hours of the morning are spent

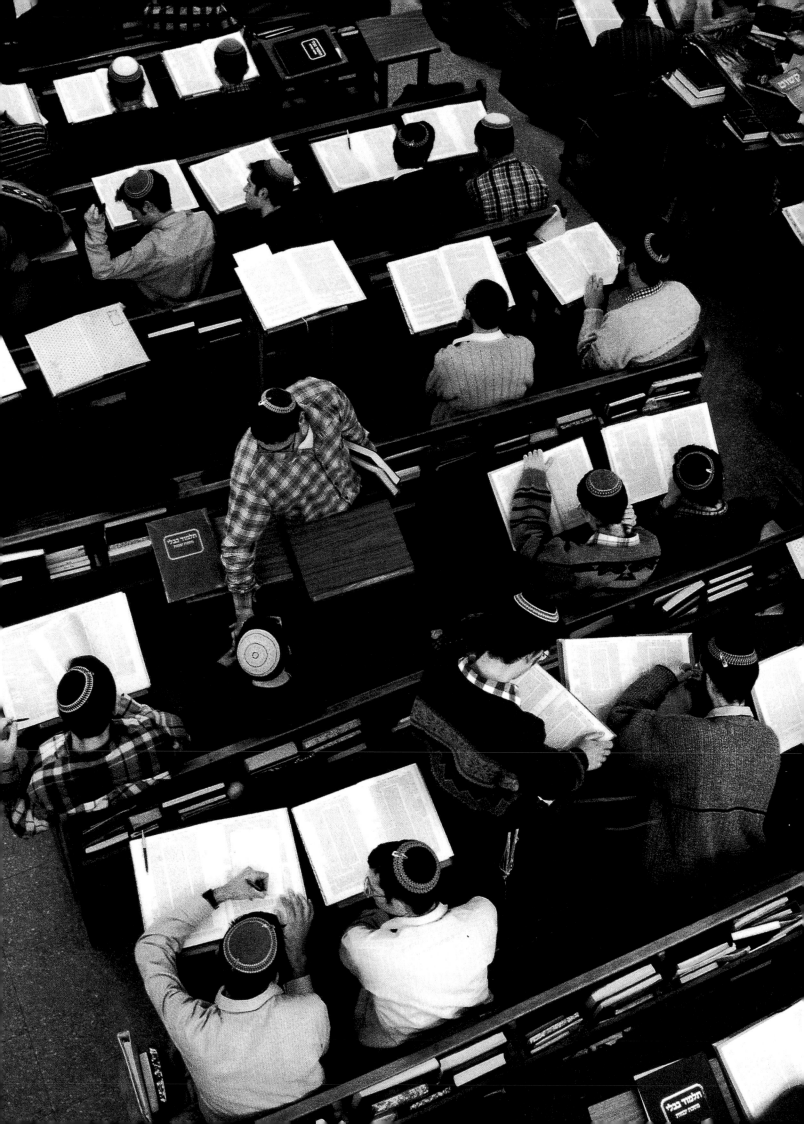

reading the texts of the *Torah*, the *Talmud* and even the *Kabbalah*.

Scriptural study is the foundation of Judaism. Setting aside time to study the *Torah* is one of the most important commandments in Jewish life.

Let us now make a brief visit inside an academy. In Hebrew, the academy is called *Beth Hamidrash* or *yeshivah*. If you are accustomed to the religious silence which normally reigns in libraries, you would be surprised by the disorderliness, brouhaha and constant comings and goings in a *Beth Hamidrash*. The academy, which also serves as a synagogue, and frequently, a dining hall or place to hold festivities, is the centre of intellectual and spiritual life. Some academies receive hundreds of students, all crowded in the same room and studying out loud at the same time.

Talmudic scholars are not monks. Silence is not a rule. Piles of books of all different sizes, opened and closed, spill over pell-mell from randomly aligned tables. Students, some sitting or standing, an occasional one with his knee resting on a bench or chair, pore over the texts of the *Talmud*. Sometimes they study side by side, but more often than not they sit facing each other. They read out loud while rocking back and forth or side to side, punctuating difficult articulations of reasoning with wide gestures of the thumb or by thumping impetuously on books, tables, even the shoulder of a study companion, known as the *Haver*. They leaf feverishly through books of commentary which they take from the shelves of the immense bookcases lining the hall.

The protagonists in this "war of meanings" are trying to understand, interpret and explain texts. Rarely in agreement with each other about the meaning of the passage being studied, these scholars go off to consult the Master who listens, explains and then calmly — at least for a moment — takes a position on the various theses propounded in this passionate dispute.

At a table a little further on, a student has fallen asleep with his arms crossed over his *Talmudic* text. Next to him, another student sips coffee and smokes a cigarette with a meditative air. Day and night hum with constant movement, the sound of voices and study in the exuberant atmosphere of the *Beth Hamidrash*.

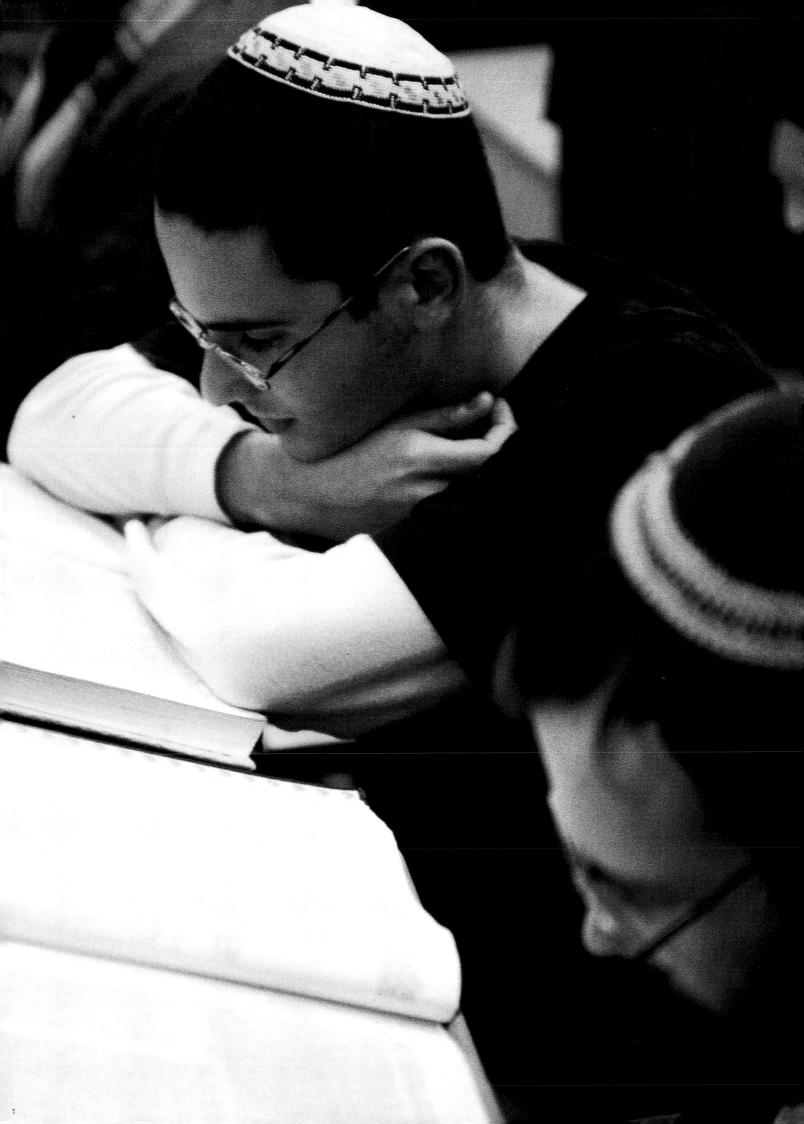

CHAPTER 21

THE DIETARY LAWS

THE LAWS IN THE *TORAH* GOVERNING *KOSHER* COOKING

ONE OF THE FUNDAMENTAL PRINCIPLES OF JUDAISM IS CALLED THE *KASHRUT*, A GENERIC TERM COVERING ALL DIETARY LAWS, SUCH AS which animals can or cannot be consumed, and which dietary combinations are forbidden (*kosher*).

Food and the culinary arts are at the root of all cultures. Cooked is to raw what culture is to nature. Nourishment is essential to humankind in that it was through the acquisition and preparation of food that man came first to speech and then to thought.

Table customs construct a body of dietary rituals which commemorate and transmit the history of a group of people. They act as a constant reminder of this history, thereby effectively ensuring the group's cohesion.

Basic Judaic dietary prohibitions concern the consumption of certain animals and the mixing of milk and meat, or milk-based foods with meat-based foods. The latter respects the commandment "Thou shalt not seethe a kid in its mother's milk". While there are numerous interpretations of this, we believe it to be a symbolic ritual that permits the separation of the mother from the child to prevent incest.

As for the first prohibition, all animals desi-gnated for consumption must be slaughtered by a person who knows the laws governing ritual slaughter (*shechitah*). This person is called the *Shochet*. Using a special knife, he slits the animals' throats. The *Shochet* then lets the blood drain out, never to be consumed. Each piece of meat is soaked in water, salted to get rid of all the blood, and finally rinsed. It is only now that the meat is fit for consumption. Blood is not consumed, as it is considered to symbolise the life and soul of the living being.

Since the Temple's destruction, the table has come to represent the altar, and the meal is one way in which the sacrifices and rituals practiced by the priests are remembered. Because of this, one should eat not only in a state of cleanliness but also purity.

It is therefore customary to wash one's hands with a special implement called a *keli* which purifies the hands before each meal at which bread is eaten; bread is considered to be a reminder of the priests' nourishment in the Temple.

With the food and words of the *kashrut*, we enter into a covenant with God. (See also the introductory chapter on the prohibition of consumption of the sciatic nerve).

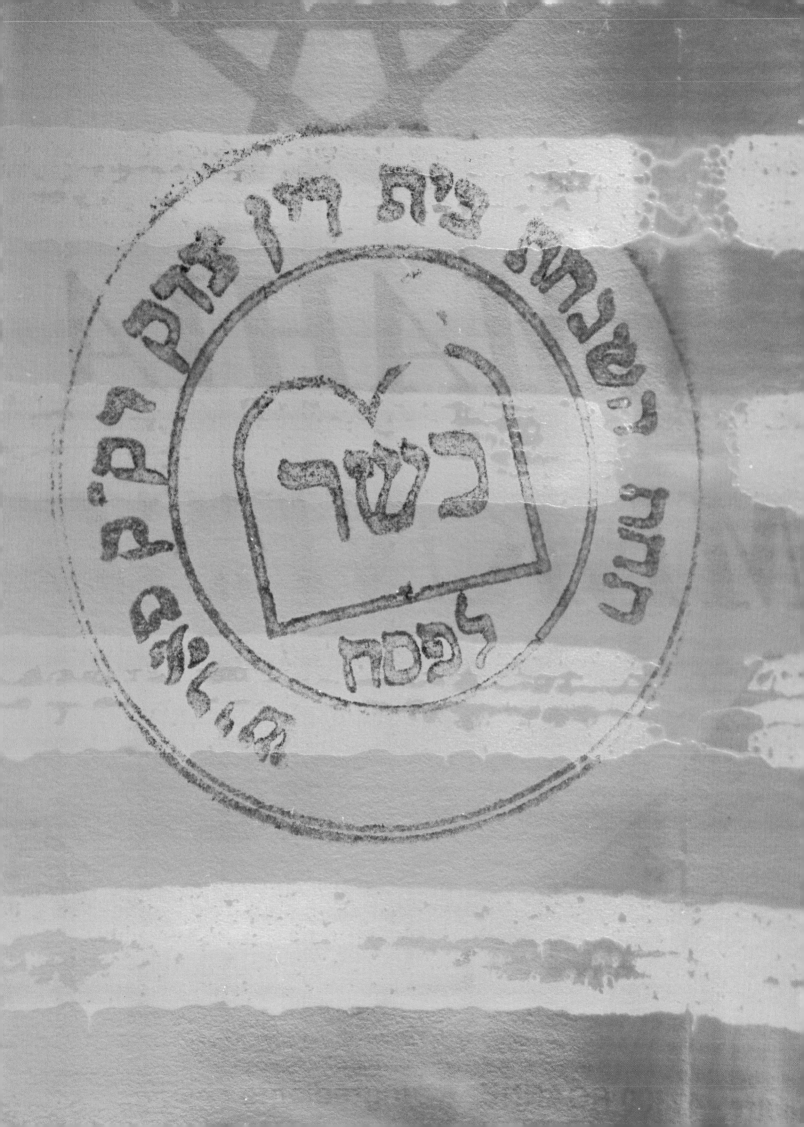

CHAPTER 22

THE MIKVEH

THE RITUAL BATH

THE *MIKVEH* IS A SMALL POOL BUILT ACCOR-DING TO PRECISE RULES. THE QUANTITY AND SOURCE OF THE WATER IT CONTAINS ARE also regulated. The *mikveh* is used to purify people and objects.

The *mikveh* must hold at least 175 gallons of water. The term *mikveh* is found in *Genesis* 1:10. "And the *mikveh* (gathering together of the waters) He called seas." The water of the *mikveh* possesses a purifying virtue. It must be natural and come either from a spring, rain, ice or snow water. Seas, rivers, lakes and reservoirs filled with rain-water are also sources of purifying water.

People and objects become unclean for a variety of reasons and they must be washed in the *mikveh*. Uncleanliness in people may be linked to death; for instance, people who have been under the same roof as a dead person are unclean.

Menstrual blood resulting from non-impre-gnation and the death of an ovule renders the female unclean. Sexual relations are forbidden during the period of uncleanliness — the period of menstruation, as well as the seven days following menstruation — and are not reauthorised until the spouse has been immersed in the *mikveh*.

The rule requiring women to abstain from sexual relations during their period of unclean-liness, and to then immerse themselves in the *mikveh* constitutes what is called the laws of familial purity (laws of *Niddah*). The immersion in the *mikveh* is called the *tevilah*.

Numerous in the time of the Temple, the occasions of purification and self-purification are now clearly fewer, but the importance of the act has not diminished.

Nowadays, the *mikveh* is frequented by women on the eve of their wedding and by mar-ried women who come to immerse themselves each time after giving birth or menstruating. People who have converted to Judaism also come to the *mikveh*.

It is visited by men on the Friday before the Sabbath as well as on the eve of *Yom Kippur*, but these visits are not obligatory. For the *Hassidim*, immersion in the *mikveh* is a mystical act of rebirth and a drawing nearer to God. Physical purity is inextricably linked to spiritual purity and so the *mikveh* is indispensable, to them and carried out with great fervour each morning before prayer.

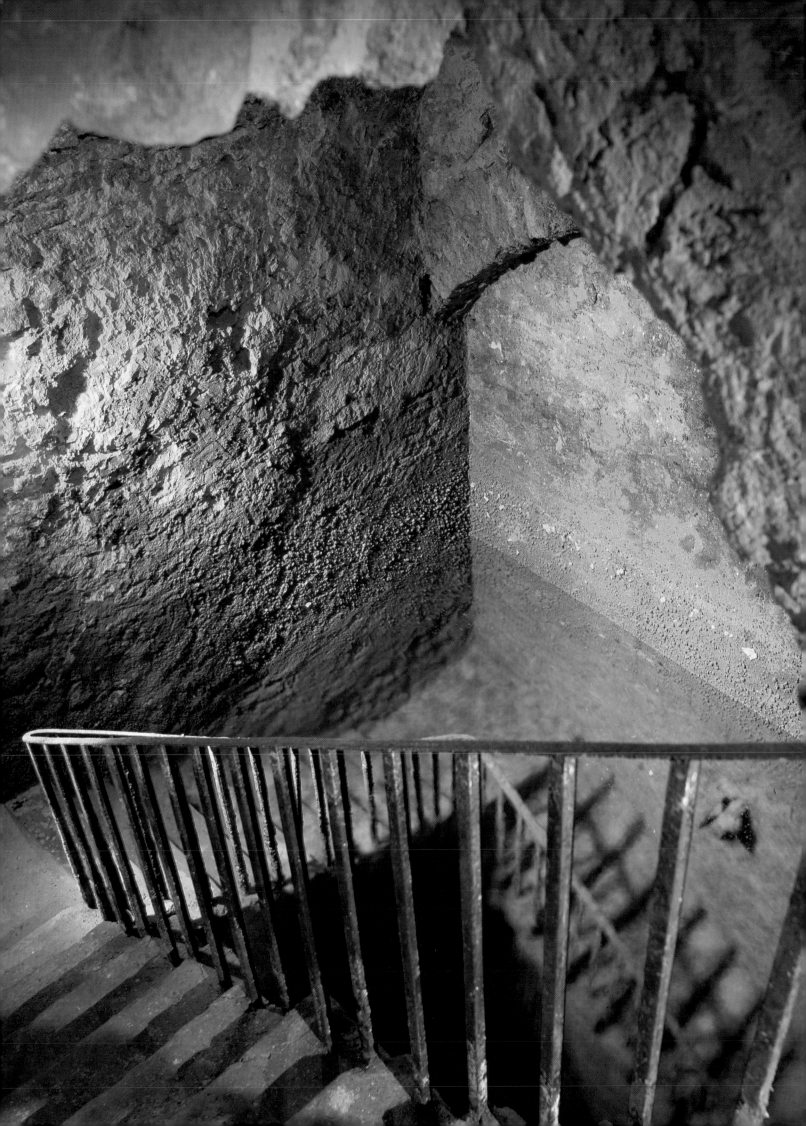

CHAPTER 23

THE HUPPAH

THE NUPTIAL CANOPY

COUPLES ARE WEDDED UNDER A NUPTIAL CANOPY CALLED THE *HUPPAH*. IN JEWISH SOCIETY, THE FAMILY, RATHER THAN THE individual, constitutes the smallest nucleus. It is an obligation stated in the *Torah* to marry and bring children into the world. The family therefore begins the day of the wedding. The symbols and customs of the wedding and nuptial canopy are numerous and very different depending on their communal origins. For example, wedding rings can be perfectly circular or outwardly slightly squared in accordance to kabbalistic custom. All marriage customs share a common goal: to bring happiness to the young couple and to wish them a fruitful marriage.

For some people, the wedding day is similar to *Kippur*, and is therefore a day of fasting, a day on which the bride and groom are purified of past mistakes and brought together, under the marriage canopy, as pure as newborn babies. The young bride-to-be immerses herself in the *mikveh* several days before the wedding so that she will be physically pure on that important day. Although the bride often wears white, it is not obligatory. This tradition, now adopted in almost every country, comes from a rabbinical law prohibiting married couples to be too richly dressed. This is so as

not to bring shame upon those who cannot afford to buy or have beautiful clothes made for their wedding. The white wedding dress is a sort of uniform which permits one to forget social disparities on that sacred day. In this way, for one day, the bride is made to feel like a true queen. The wedding ceremony is generally conducted under the marriage canopy by a rabbi who recites two benedictions from the *erusin* or *Kiddushin* over a cup of wine. The two fiancés drink from the cup and then the *Hassan* slips a ring on the index finger of the right hand of the *Kallah* while reciting the appropriate sentence. After this, the *ketubbah* or marriage contract is read. In many weddings, this is also the time for speeches. This is followed by the ceremony of the *Nissu'in* in which the seven marriage benedictions are pronounced over a second cup of wine. The wedding is usually concluded with a gesture commemorating the destruction of the Temple of Jerusalem: the young *Hassan* crushes a glass under his foot. The young newlyweds are then brought to a private room where they are left alone for a few moments to symbolise their new intimacy.

The week after the wedding is a period of rejoicing during which a feast ending with the seven marriage blessings is held each day.

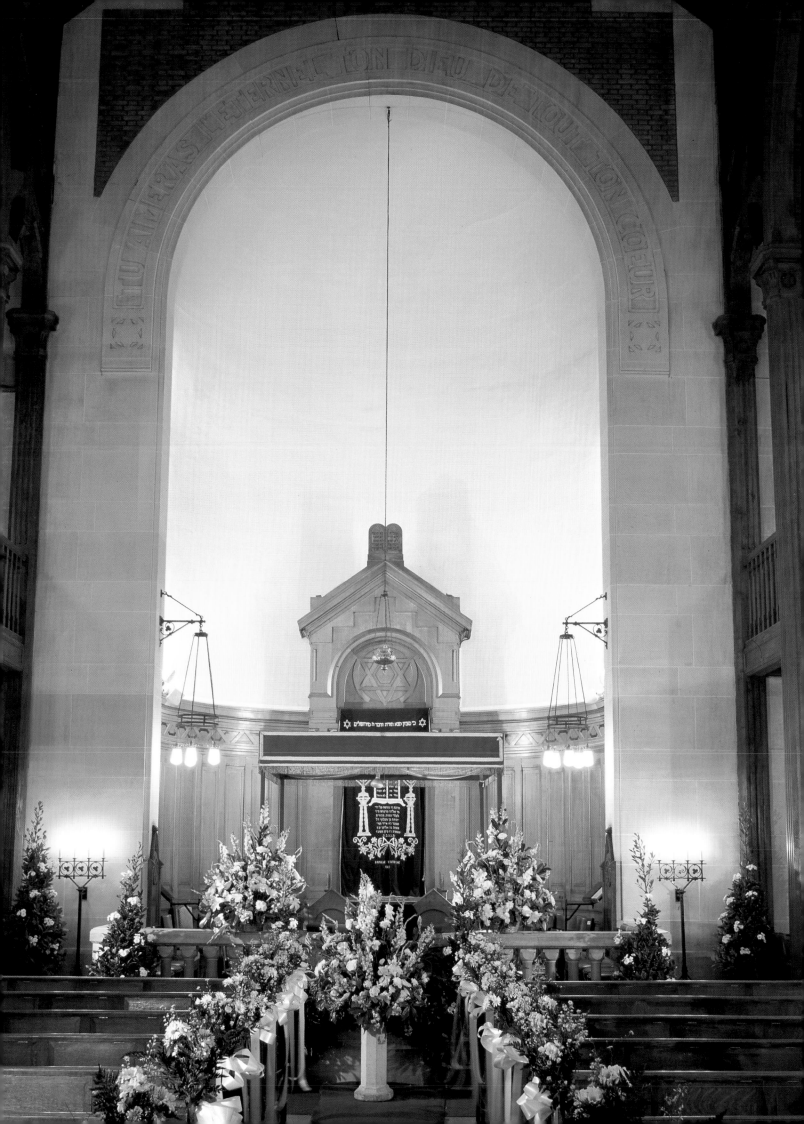

CHAPTER 24

THE KETUBBAH

THE MARRIAGE CONTRACT

UNDER THE *HUPPAH*, THE RABBI OR PERSON CONDUCTING THE WEDDING CEREMONY PUTS BEFORE THE BRIDE AND GROOM (THE *HASSAN* and the *Kallah*) a "marriage act", the *ketubbah*. Literally, the word *ketubbah* means "that which is written", an abbreviation of the expression "written commitment".

The *ketubbah*, which is inaccurately translated as a marriage contract is, in fact, a divorce insurance. It guarantees that in the event of an official separation the husband will give the wife enough money to live on for several years, for however much time it takes her to find a stable situation. It is a standard legal document which is signed by the future husband in the presence of two witnesses before the wedding and given to the young wife during the ceremony.

Written in Aramaic, this document enumerates the husband's obligations, especially financial, to his wife on a daily basis and in the case of a divorce. The oldest existing *ketubbah*, found in the south of Egypt, goes back to the fifth century of the pre-common era.

For two essential reasons, it inspired the art of calligraphy, illustration and manuscript illumination. The *ketubbah* is not subject to any restrictions concerning its binding, nor to its size, shape or lettering. It is associated with marriage, which is, by definition, a joyous occasion. Therefore, all patterns, colours, techniques and innovations are permitted.

The problem of the *ketubbah* occupies a privileged place in Talmudic law. An entire treatise entitled *Ketubot* details all the legal formulations in the writing of the *ketubbah*. So many points of law are discussed concerning this matter that the *Ketubot* treatise has been called *Shas Katan*: the miniature *Talmud*.

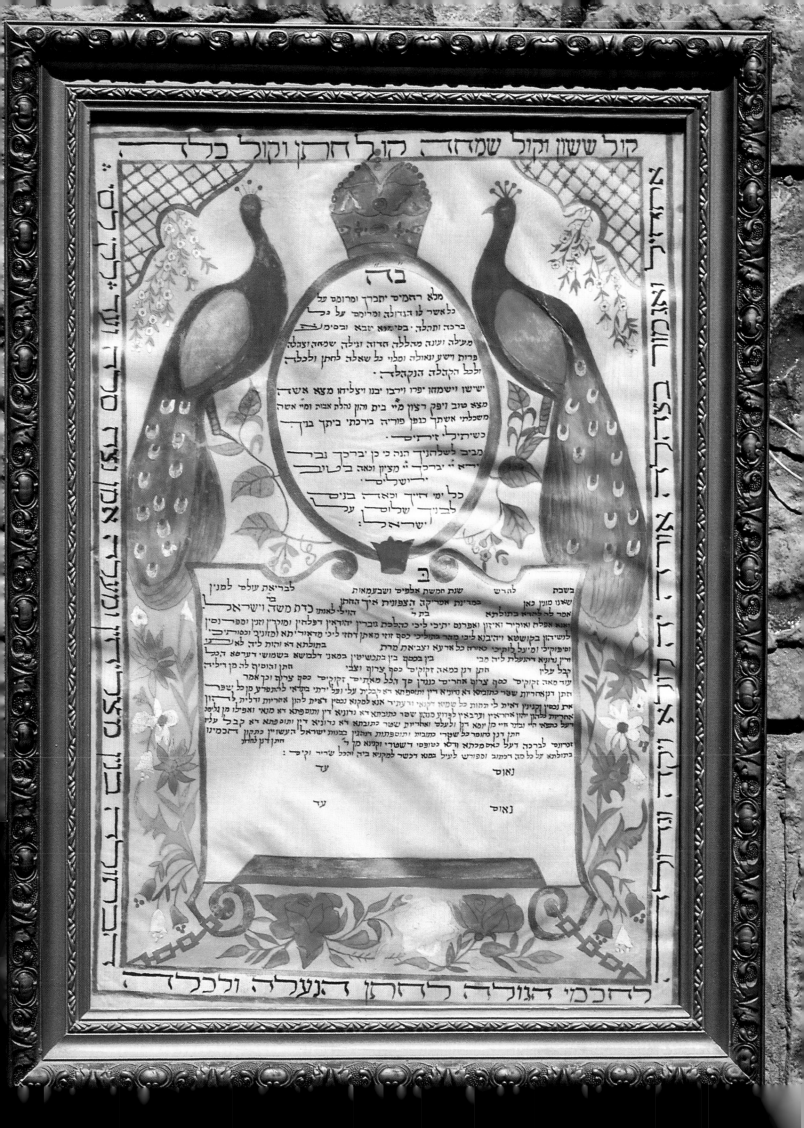

CHAPTER 25

THE BRIT MILAH

CIRCUMCISION

THE WORD *MILAH* IS DERIVED FROM BOTH THE HEBREW VERB "TO CUT"AND THE VERB "TO BE FACE TO FACE". IT IS MAY ALSO BE CONNECTED to the root of the Hebrew verb "to speak".

Circumcision is a way of introducing language into the body and bringing the body of the infant into the sphere of language. Circumcision is a sign of the convenant between God and the Hebrew people. Despite persecution, it is one of the obligations that Jews have observed over their entire anguished history. It involves the removal of the foreskin from the penis of a baby boy on the eighth day by a *Mohel*, specialised in this type of procedure. It is at this time that the infant is given his name or names.

According to the scriptures, Abraham was the first person to be circumcised. He was 99 years old at the time. His son, Ishmael, the father of Islam, was circumcised at the age of thirteen, and this is why Moslems circumcise boys at this age. Isaac was circumcised when he was eight days old, and this came to be the rule for later generations of Jews.

The ceremony can take place on any day of the week including the Sabbath or even *Kippur*. But if the infant is too small or is jaundiced, the *milah* is considered dangerous and is postponed until the baby is out of danger. At the moment of circumcision, the baby is placed on a special high-chair called the"Chair of the prophet Elijah" as, traditionally, the prophet Elijah is invited to each circumcision.

The *Mohel* uses ancient instruments: a double-edged knife, a stylet or probe which detaches the foreskin from the gland, and the *magen* (shield) which protects the gland during the incision. The ceremony ends with the giving of the blessing specific to circumcision, followed by a *seudah* or feast.

Gentiles are also circumcised when they convert. If they are already circumcised, it is sufficient to spill a drop of blood.

We believe that the incompleteness rendered by circumcision enables human beings to enter into the dimension of language. Circumcision removes a part of the man so that he will experience a sense of loss or incompleteness. This leads him to reconstruct and reinvent himself. Obviously, one would ask, "What is the form of circumcision for females?" In the dialectical relationship between man and woman, the woman already carries this loss which inscribes her in the dynamic of desire. She does not therefore need to be circumcised.

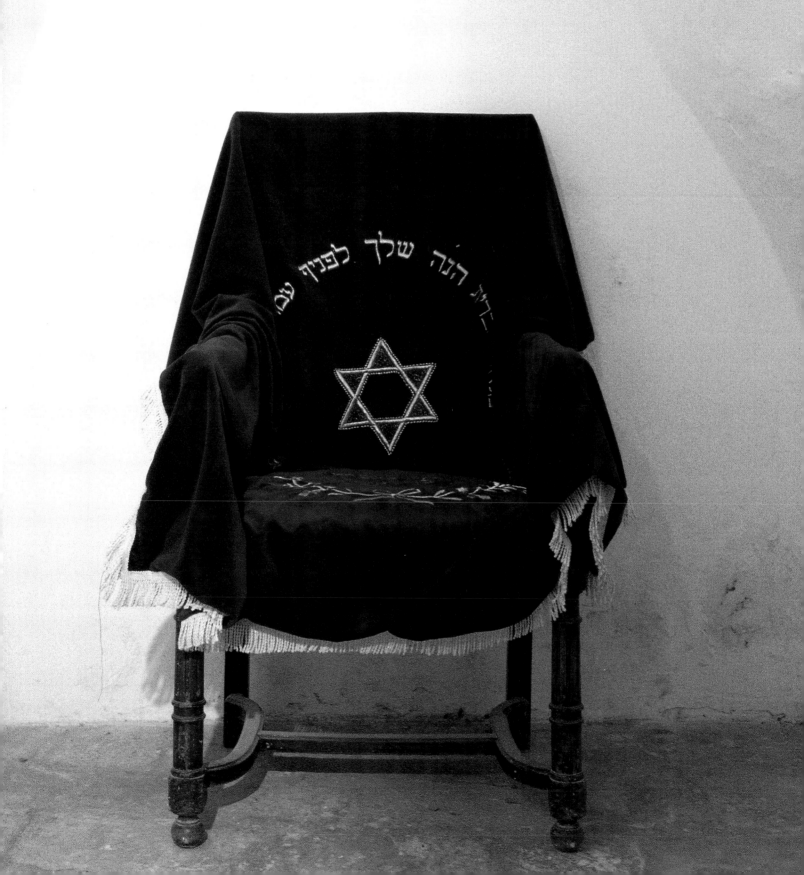

CHAPTER 26

THE BAR-MITZVAH

AND THE *BAT-MITZVAH*:
THE RELIGIOUS AGE OF MAJORITY

THE AGE OF MAJORITY IN JUDAISM IS THIRTEEN FOR BOYS AND TWELVE FOR GIRLS. THIS JOYOUS AND FESTIVE OCCASION MARKS a very important step in the life of an adolescent.

At thirteen, a Jewish boy achieves the status of a responsible adult from a religious point of view. Literally, *Bar-Mitzvah* means "son of the commandment": from this moment on, the child will come under all the obligations of manhood and is held responsible for his acts but also transgressions.

The closest Monday or Thursday to the thirteenth birthday in the Hebrew calendar is the occasion for religious celebrations. On this day of great ceremony, the young boy performs certain rituals for the first time in his life.

First of all, he wears the *tefillin* to the synagogue and prays there for the first time. Now that the boy has reached the age of majority, he can be a member of the *minyan*, the *quorum* of ten men required to say a prayer together. On the Sabbath following the *Bar-Mitzvah*, the boy says the morning or evening service before the entire community. In the morning, he is called upon to read from the *Torah*, and it is customary to read all or a portion of the week's parashah (see the chapter on the scrolls of the *Torah*).

A *seudah* is held on the Sabbath or during the week. Throughout this ritual meal, the young *Bar-Mitzvah* delivers a speech to demonstrate his capacity to grasp the subtlety of the commentaries on traditional texts.

For girls, there is a ceremony called *Bat-Mitzvah* which takes place on the twelfth instead of the thirteenth birthday. This is because girls are considered to mature faster than boys. It is only recently that the *Bat-Mitzvah* has also become the occasion of a celebration. Nevertheless, although traditions are slowly changing, this has not yet become a general rule.

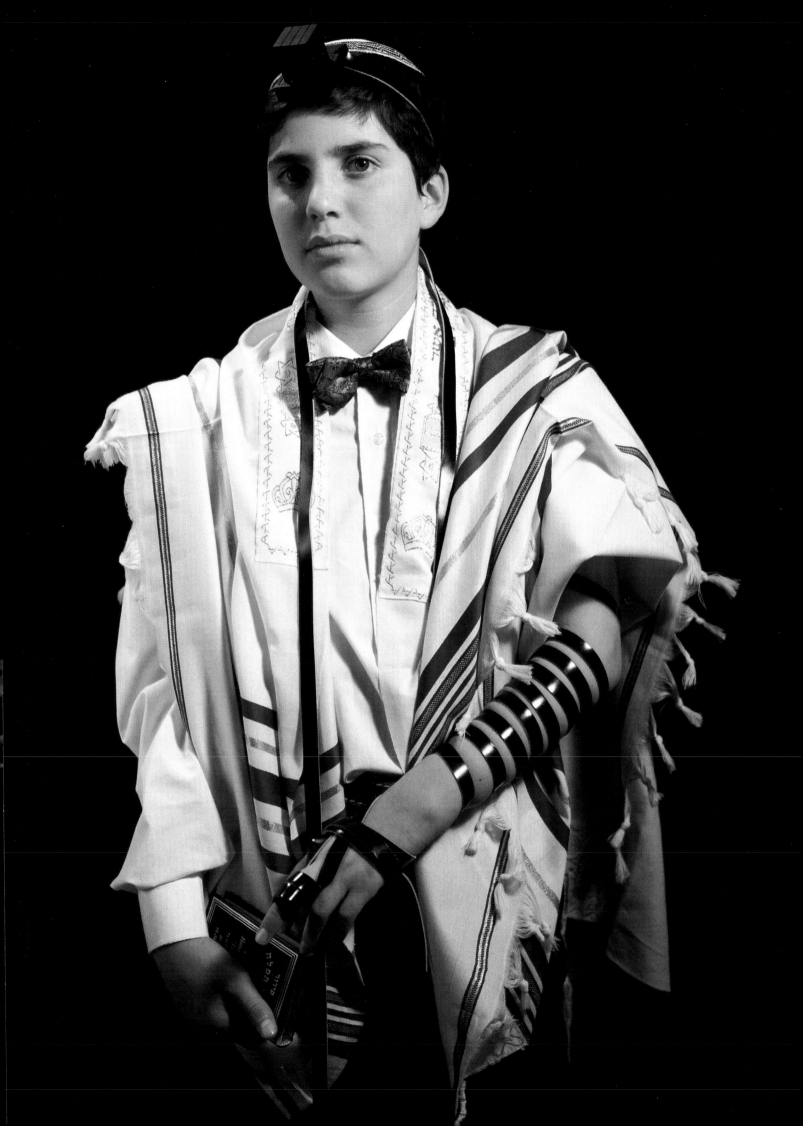

CHAPTER 27

THE CLOTHING CUSTOMS

HATS, BEARDS, LOCKS, WIGS AND SCARVES

WITH THE EXCEPTION OF THE *TALLITH* AND THE *TEFILLIN*, WHICH ARE OBLIGATORY AND ESSENTIALLY THE SAME FOR ALL JEWS, clothing customs vary from country to country.

Some Jews of Eastern European origin, such as the *Hassidim*, observe eighteenth-century clothing customs: black coats, high socks, and fur-trimmed, wide-brimmed hats called *shtreimel*.

Other Jews from the same region but disciples of different masters always wear black jackets and trousers, with white shirts and Borsalino-type hats inherited from turn-of-the-century fashion styles. Certain clothes are only worn on special occasions, such as the long, white robe which drapes the officiating minister on *Yom Kippur* and recalls the dress of the High Priest during the time of the Temple.

The origin of the wearing of beards and sidelocks (called *pe'ot* in Hebrew and *payess* in Yiddish), lies in a biblical prohibition of the use of any cutting or slicing objects on the face. Symbolically, this signifies that man's face must not be aggressed, that violence must not be done to the humanity of man.

For women, the emphasis is on modesty Tseniuth. She should, of course, be dressed in a modest fashion, but above all, she must keep her head covered.

The head may be covered by a scarf, as do North African women, by a wig or *shaytl*, which women from Eastern Europe wear, or even a beret or small hat for more modern young women.

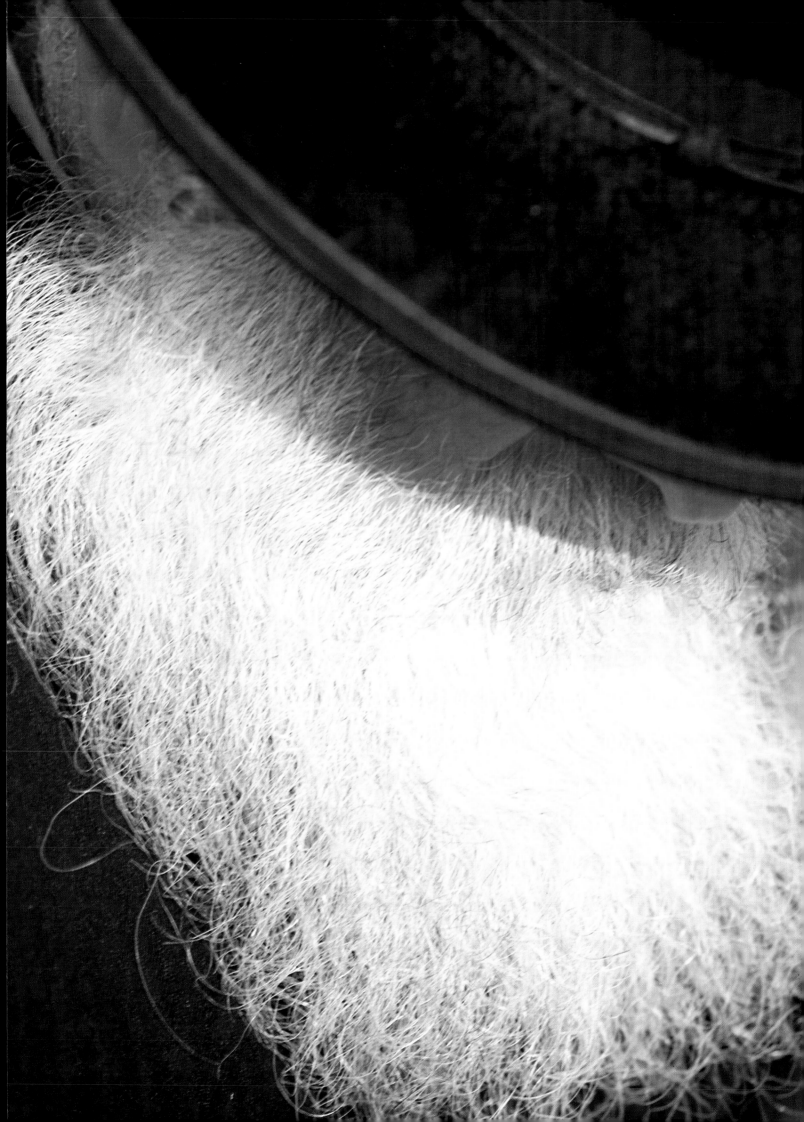

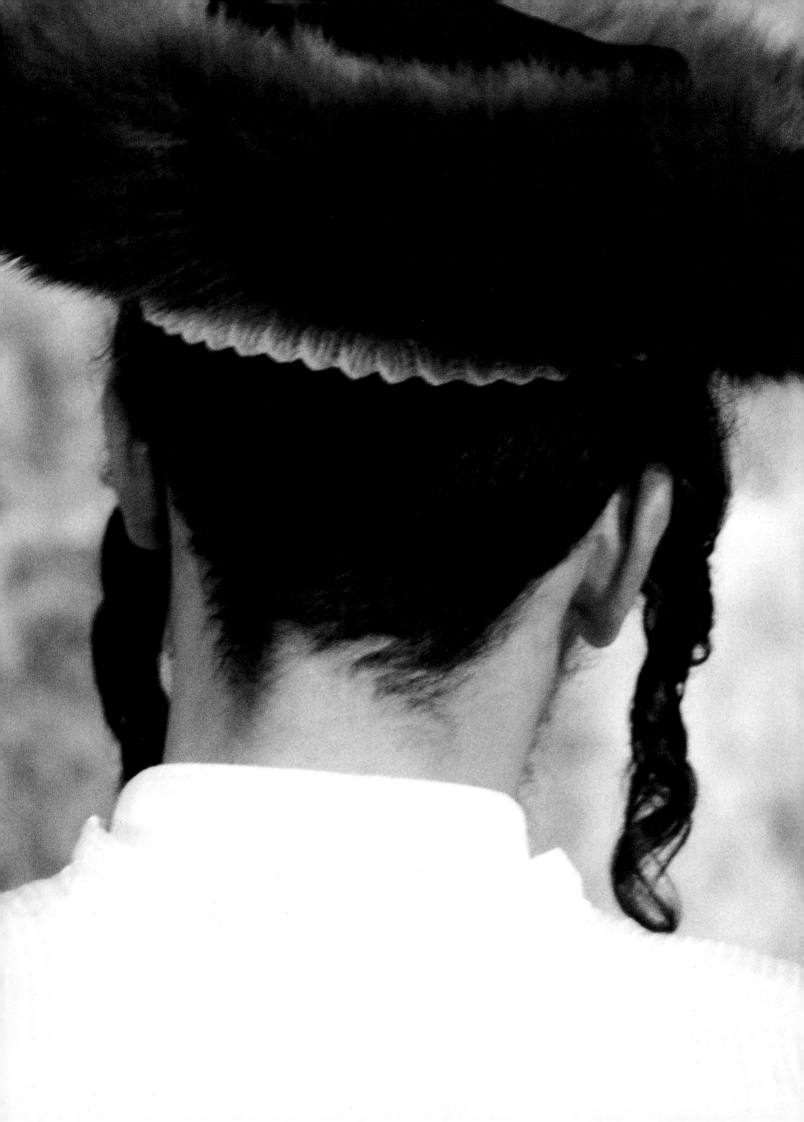

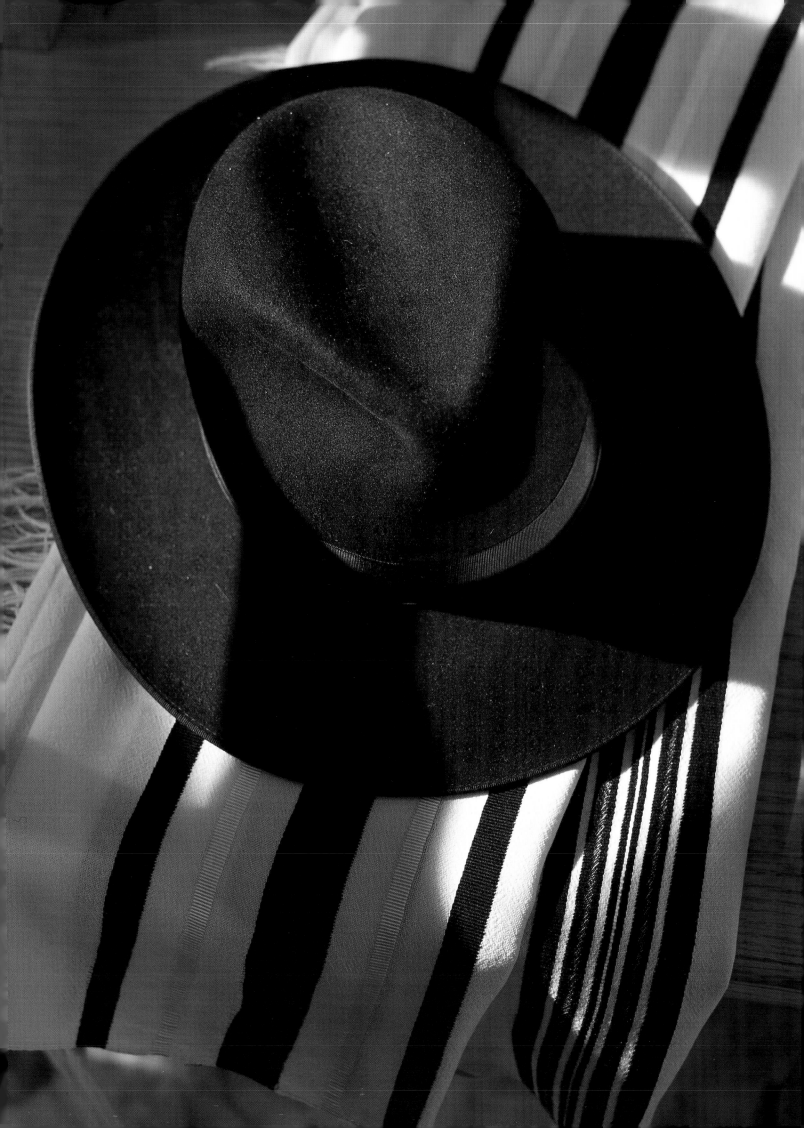

CHAPTER 28

THE KIPPAH

A SMALL, EMBROIDERED
OR PLAIN CLOTH SKULL-CAP WHICH MEN
WEAR ON THEIR HEADS

THE SHAPE AND SIZE OF THE *KIPPAH*, OFTEN REFERRED TO AS THE *YARMULKA*, DIFFERS DEPENDING ON THE COMMUNITY. IN THE Braslav communities (mystic Jews originating from Russia), the *kippah* is very wide and covers the whole head. It is embroidered, white or cream-coloured and has a little pompon on the top. In Orthodox Sephardic communities (originating from Spain and Portugal and their descendants), the *kippah* is worn under a black hat and is clearly smaller than the Braslavian *kippah*. It is also embroidered but black in colour.

In Orthodox Ashkenazic communities of German or Eastern European origins, the *kippah* is also worn under a black hat but is made of black cloth. In non-Orthodox communities who accept modernity and are, in general, zionists, that is, who recognise the legitimacy and centrality of the state of Israel, the *kippah* is embroidered and can be of any colour. In reality, the *Torah* states no obligation regarding the wearing of the *kippah*; rather, it is a custom which has become obligatory through the passing of time.

Since the eighteenth century, the *kippah*, which has gradually replaced the turban among Sephardic Jews and the large hats among the Ashkenazim, has become a sign of piety and Jewish identity. The exact meaning of the *kippah* is not known; above all it is a sign of man's humility in his relationship to God.

Man may place a symbolic limit above his head as a sign of his finite nature. But the *kippah* can also be seen as the necessity of placing a limit above one self in order to overcome and go beyond it.

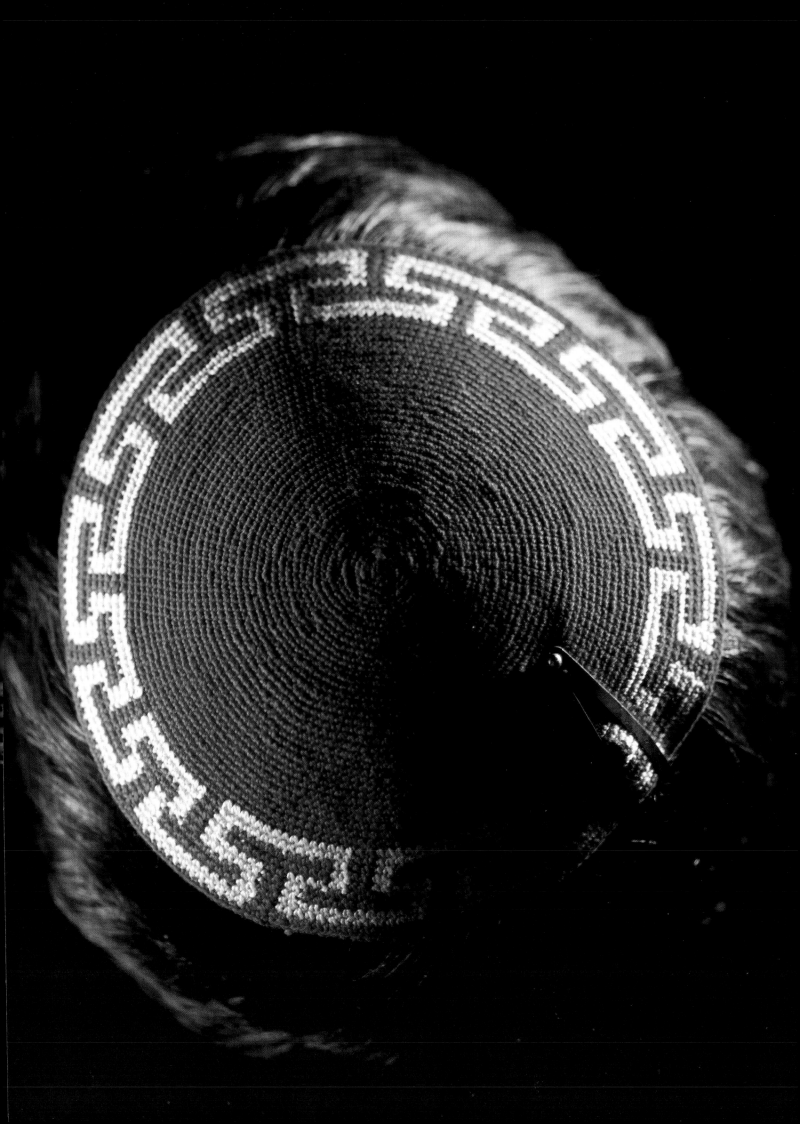

CHAPTER 29

THE TEMPLE

AND ITS MEMORY:
THE WESTERN OR
WAILING WALL.
THE *KOTEL*.

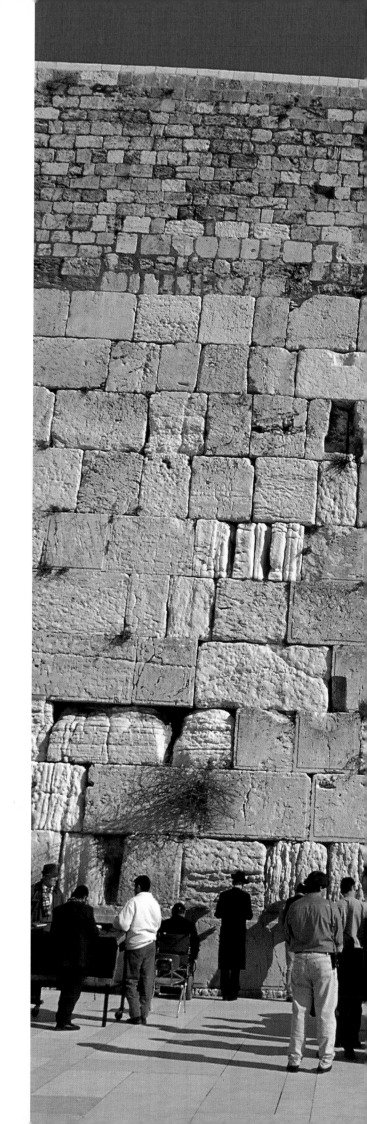

SINCE THE BEGINNING OF TIME, MAN HAS
NEEDED SPECIFIC PLACES FOR WORSHIP AND
PRAYER. THE FIRST HEBREWS BUILT AN ARK,
or *Mishkan*, (house of God), which accompanied
them during the forty years in the desert. Later,
this travelling temple was replaced by a more
durable one built by King Solomon.

Built on Mount Moriah in Jerusalem, the
Temple is the House of God, the centre of worship for the Jewish people.

King Solomon had the first Temple built in
the tenth century of the pre-common era on one
of Jerusalem's hills, Mount Moriah, acquired by
his father, King David, for this very purpose. The
construction lasted seven years and resulted in a
sumptuous building which housed the Holy of
Holies and the Holy Ark, the incense altar of
perfumes and the Golden Candlestick, as well as
many other cult-objects which Solomon added.

The Temple was 60 cubits long (8 feet), 20
cubits wide (2,5 feet), and 30 cubits in height (4
feet). It had a high portico, sculpted cedar-panel-

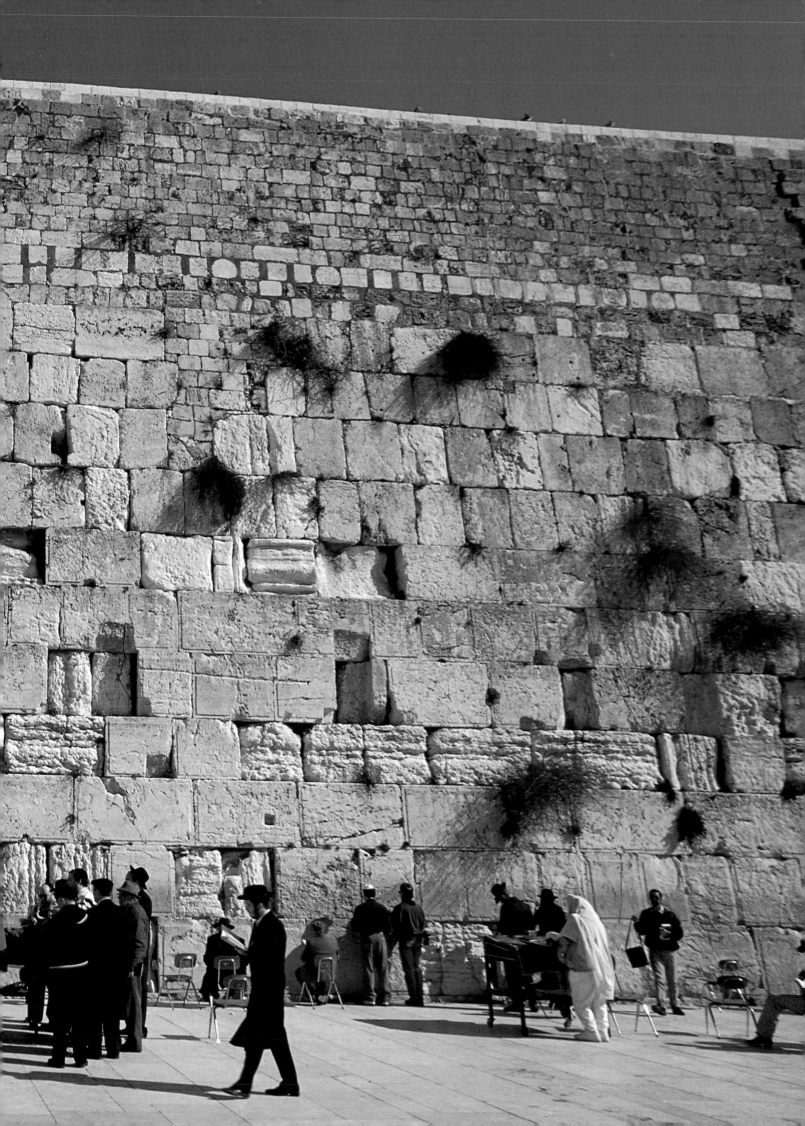

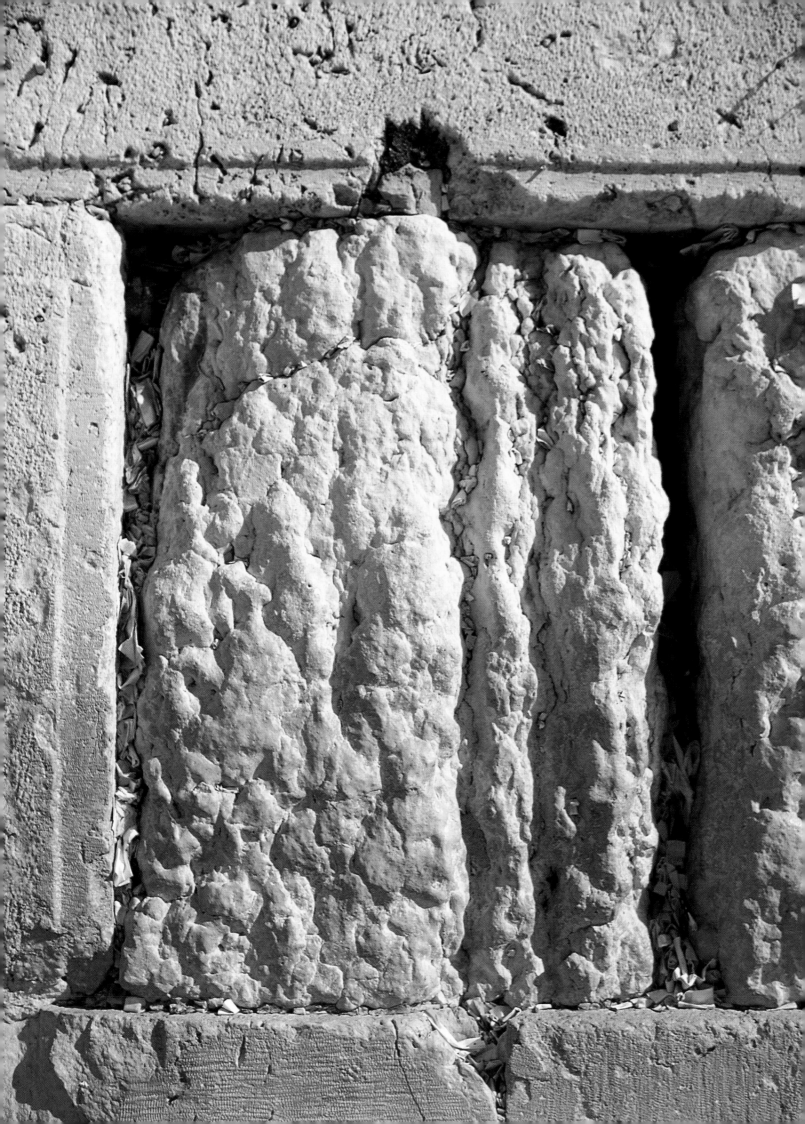

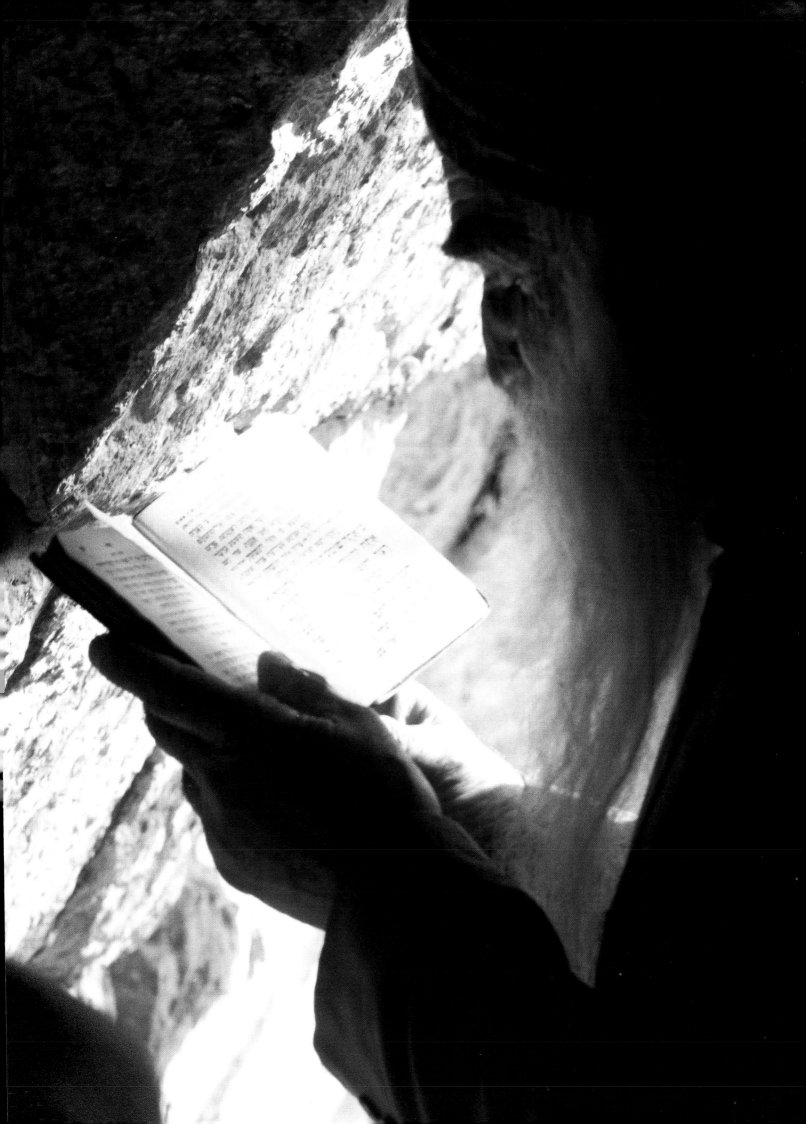

led walls and solidly-barred windows. The Ark of the Covenant was reached through a cyprus and olive-wood door covered in gold. In the Holy of Holies, the most sacred place in the House of God, cherubim with outspread wings, colocynths and flowers in bloom were carved out of cedar and olive-wood and covered in a layer of pure gold.

The floor, walls, and ceiling were also covered in gold. On the two bronze pillars at the entrance of the Temple, Solomon had the word *Jachin* engraved on the pillar on the right and *Boaz* on the pillar on the left.

During King Solomon's reign, the Temple was the centre of worship. Daily sacrifices were made there, as well as all Sabbath and festival sacrifices. And three times a year, during the pilgrimage festivals, the entire population would go the Temple to offer the sacrifice specific to the festival. After King Solomon died, the kingdom was divided and the central role of the Temple diminished considerably.

The first Temple was destroyed in 586 of the pre-common era by Nebuchadnezzar. Ezra and Nehemiah had it rebuilt and it was inaugurated in 516 pre-common era. The second Temple, which Herod had restored and expanded, was destroyed in year 70 by Titus and his Roman army.

According to tradition, the first Temple was destroyed as a result of idolatry, incest and blood crimes and the second, because of gratuitous hate among the Jews. The anniversary of the destruction of the two Temples on the 9th of the month of *Ab*, is a day of great mourning and fasting for the Jewish people.

The masters of the tradition had the foresight to build another Temple immediately after the destruction of the second — an invisible temple of spirit and study. It is the creation of Rabbi Yochanan ben Zakkai, who asked one thing of Vespasian when he became Roman emperor: "Permit me to build a school in the city of Yavne". Thus was constructed an "invisible building" which could never be destroyed, a living culture constantly renewed through the reading of texts and the infinite movement of their commentaries.

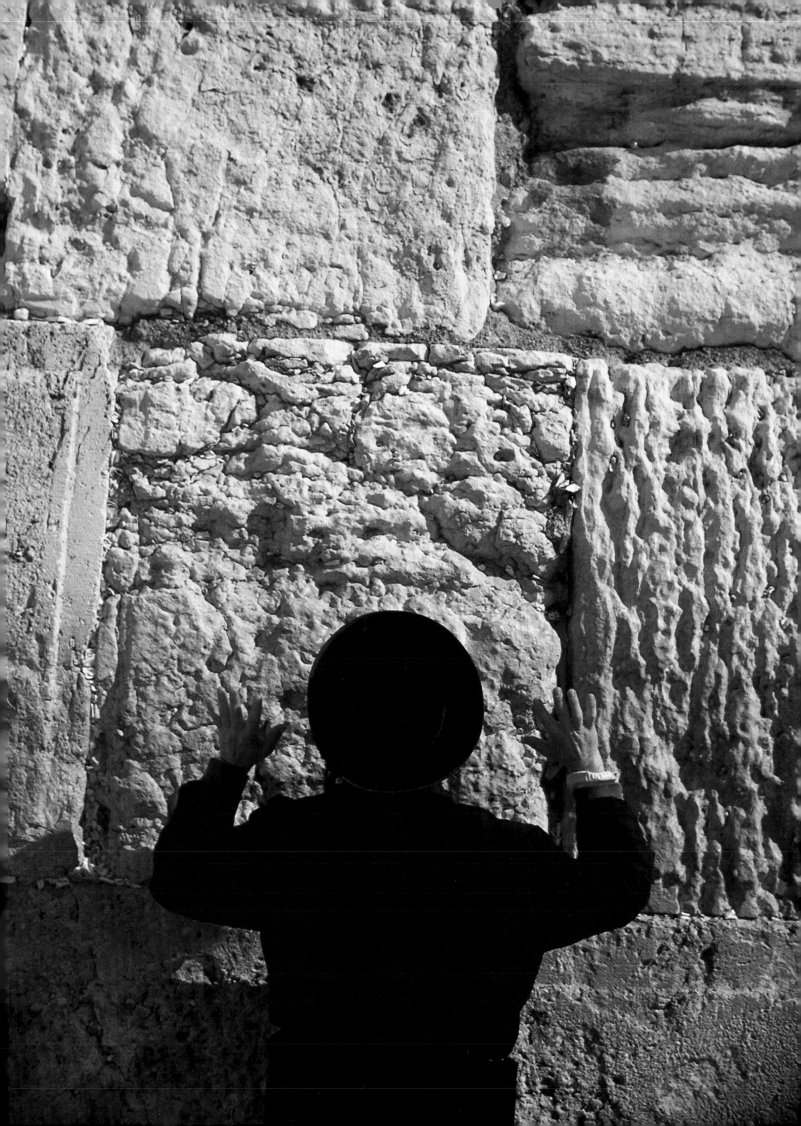

CHAPTER 30

THE MAGEN DAVID

THE STAR OF DAVID

THE *MAGEN DAVID* OR STAR OF DAVID IS THE MOST WIDELY-KNOWN SYMBOL OF JUDAISM. LITERALLY, *MAGEN DAVID* MEANS "SHIELD OF David". It is a geometric sign formed by two inter-twined, equilateral triangles.

This symbol, often inscribed in a circle, was common to many peoples several centuries before the common era.

It was not until the fourteenth century that this geometric motif was definitively associated with the expression "Magen David" in a kabbalistic work.

Generally, its purpose was to provide protection from demons and evil spirits and has only very recently become the symbol of the Jewish people. It now appears on all sorts of cult-objects, from Europe to the confines of Russia.

In his book, *Star of Redemption*, Franz Rosenzweig attributes an essential idea to each point of the star: Creation, Redemption and Revelation, Humanity, the world, and God.

In 1897, the first Zionist congress chose the *Magen David* as its emblem and it later became the centre motif of the Israeli flag; the much more ancient and authentic menorah symbolises the state. In his book, *Jewish Messianism*, Gershom Scholem argues that the sanctity of an authentic living symbol has been conferred upon the *Magen David* by the segregation and degradation, the annihilation, the humiliation and the horror which drove millions of people marked with this yellow star to the gas chambers.

Under this sign, the Jews were assassinated and under this same sign, which has become worthy of illuminating the path to life and recons-truction, the Jews have become reunited in Israel. It is precisely because of the ultimate humiliation, suffering and terrifying finality with which this symbol has become so charged that it has acquired such noble title and bearing.

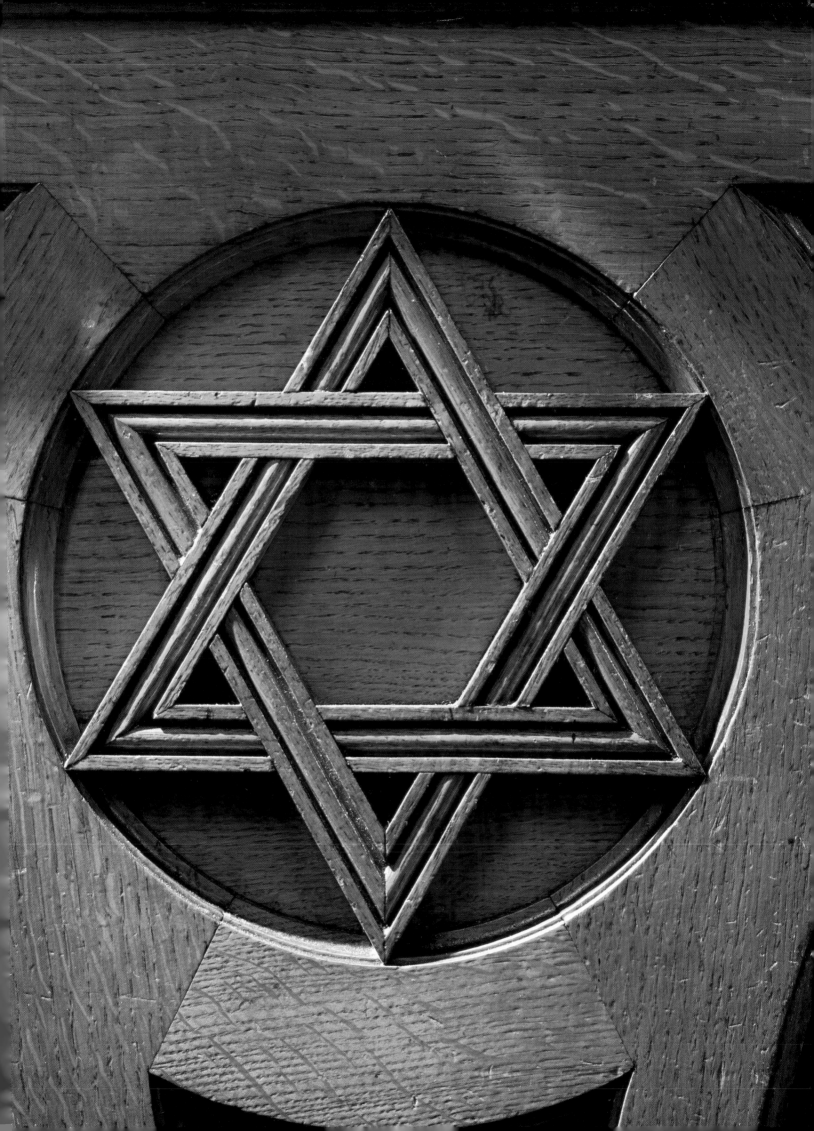

ACKNOWLEDGEMENTS

I would like, first of all, to thank my wife, Dory Rotnemer, whose effective presence, precious help and judicious advice sustained us throughout this passionate work. This book would never have been possible without the discrete and efficient work of Philippe Sebirot, assistant-photographer to Laziz Hamani. It is with great joy that I thank all those who helped us produce this work by opening doors to us and putting art and traditional pieces, often collection items, at our disposal. We would particularly like to thank M. Elie Partouche, treasurer of the synagogal community of rue Chasseloup-Laubat and the rabbi of this synagogue, Rabbi Maurice Nezri. Also, Emilie and Guy Fellous who so devotedly oversee this synagogue. In this synagogue, we photographed a man praying with *tallith*, *tzitzith*, and *tefillin*. We also photographed the *mezuzah*, the Holy Ark, the *Sefer Torah*, the *Sefer* hand, the *mappah* and the *sefer* ornaments, the *megillah* and the *huppah*. The *David magen* (page 125) shows a chair from the synagogue. Access to the synagogue of Carpentras was made possible by Jacques Ouaknin, Chief Rabbi of Marseilles. We thank the entire team. We also particularly thank the president of the community of Carpentras where we photographed the beautiful synagogue (page 33) and the *mikveh* (page 103). Chief Rabbi Max Warschavski and Madame very generously loaned us several collection objects such as the *Seder* and *Hannukah* dishes. We warmly thank them both. We especially thank Rav Eliahou Zohar who so kindly opened the doors of his studio to us. The photo on the cover was taken in his studio in Jerusalem. We would also like to express our gratitude to the Hasidim of the Yeshivah Braslav for their hospitality. The photos of the *yeshivah* were taken at the Mercaz Harav Kook Yeshivah in Jerusalem. We thank the shopowners and antique storeowners in Paris and Jerusalem for allowing us to use their artefacts.

– The Alexander store on Ben Yehouda street who put the Sabbath candlesticks, *Havdalah* objects and the Ketubbah at our disposal.

– The store Diasporama who lent us the *kiddush* glass.

We would also like to express our gratitude to the Prunelle studios for having so graciously allowed us to use their space. The photos of the *succah* and *lulav* were taken at the Rambam synagogue in Paris' 17th arrondissement. The *purim* costumes were offered by Mme Amsilli from Marseille to whom we extend our deepest gratitude. The *Haggadot* in the photograph (page 87) were graciously put at our disposal by M. and Mme. Max Assouline and M. Ernest Assouline. We warmly thank them. The synagogue (page 50) is that of Rabbi Yochanan ben Zakkai in the Jewish quarter in old Jerusalem. The *Eliahou Hanavi* chair was found in an adjoining room to the synagogue. The photographs of the tombs were taken at the Mount of Olives facing old Jerusalem. Finally, I join Laziz Hamani in thanking Mr. Momi Boussidan who permitted the doors of the synagogue on rue Rambam to be opened to us. We would also like to thank the Consistoire de Paris (L'ACIP), Publimod Photo laboratory and Daniel Delisle Studio for producing this book.